Nurturing Reflexive Practice

in

Higher Education

Educators Engaged in Action Research Projects in an
Institution of Higher Learning in Kenya

Edited by

Faith Maina

Nsemia

First Edition: August 2014
Published by Nsemia Inc. Publishers (www.nsemia.com)

Edited By: Faith Maina
Cover Concept Illustration: Peter Murumba
Cover Design: Danielle Pitt
Layout Design: Kemunto Matunda
Production Consultant: Matunda Nyanchama

Note for Librarians:
A cataloguing record for this book is available from Library and Archives Canada.

ISBN: 978-1-926906-37-9 Paperback

DEDICATION

This work is dedicated to Ambrose Chedotum, a valuable member of this cohort whose life was prematurely cut short a few days after the completion of the course out of which this collection of papers arose. May you rest in eternal peace!

ACKNOWLEDGEMENTS

In 2011, I applied and obtained a Fulbright Award to teach a course on *Research, Writing and Dissemination for Academics & Professionals* at Moi University in Eldoret, Kenya. In my proposal statement, I had indicated that having been an editor, associate editor, member of editorial boards and reviewer for academic journals for many years, I had witnessed first-hand the struggles many young Kenyan academic professionals experience in writing research articles for academic journals. The consequence was that few got published in academic journals and even when some eventually got published, their research was already dated. Moreover, most manuscripts ended up being rejected even though the data produced had significant implications for policy development and the local population. The young academics therefore stagnated professionally because most promotions in academic institutions require a certain number of publications in peer-refereed journals. A serious consequence is that a country like Kenya becomes a nation of knowledge consumers, which undermines its ability to be a producer of knowledge.

This book grew out of this course that lasted 10 months from September 2011 to May 2012. The course was conceptualized through synergistic discussions with Dr. Wanjiku Khamasi, the then Director of the Institute of Gender, Research and Development (IGERD) at Moi University. In her official letter of invitation, Dr. Khamasi indicated that "research is central to IGERD's capacity building initiatives. Our young academics and professionals lack adequate skills to write research for an academic audience. By improving the skills, resources and knowledge in research writing and dissemination, Dr. Maina will help us meet one of our 2007-2012 strategic plans."

I would therefore like to thank the United States Council for the International Exchange of Scholars, the administrator of the Fulbright Scholars Program for granting me this opportunity to travel, live and work in Kenya for a period of 10 months. Kenya is the country where I was born and raised, therefore, my Fulbright visit was a home-coming event in many ways. I'm forever grateful to Moi

University and specifically, to Dr. Wanjiku Khamasi, who tirelessly worked to prepare for my visit, provided me with office and meeting space, and registered 15 young academic professionals for my class. Moi University provided me with room and board, and thankfully, I got a chance to meet and fraternize with many visitors, courtesy of being housed at the institution.

Many thanks to my home institution, State University of New York, (SUNY) Oswego for supporting and inspiring me to pursue the Fulbright Award. Specifically, many thanks to the then chair of my Department of Curriculum and Instruction, Dr. Pam Michel, who as always supported me throughout the process of application and after. I was pleased to note that SUNY Oswego was named by the Chronicle of Higher Education as a top-producing Fulbright Campus that year.

To the authors of the chapters that follow, many thanks for starting and walking the journey to the very end. Thank you for your commitment to the project, especially attending those evening classes with dedication even though you had all your other day duties and responsibilities. This could not have been possible without your professionalism and patience.

Special thanks to members of my immediate and extended family for emotional support and love. To my children, Muraguri and Waruguru thank you for being my anchors. I'm forever grateful and appreciative of your love.

Faith Maina

TABLE OF CONTENTS

CHAPTER ONE

Nurturing Reflexive Practice

Faith Maina

SECTION ONE

CHALLENGES EXPERIENCED BY COLLEGE STUDENTS

CHAPTER TWO

Unplanned Pregnancies and Barriers to Use of Contraception Among College Female Students in Kenyan Public Universities

Rachel L. Karei

CHAPTER THREE

Challenges Affecting the Academic Performance of Female Commuter Students at a Public University in Uasin Gishu County, Kenya

Felicity Wanjiru Githinji

CHAPTER FOUR

Challenges and Barriers to Quality Education for Student Mothers in Kenya's Public Universities

Mary Mahugu

CHAPTER FIVE

Examination Cheating in Public Institutions of Higher Learning in Kenya

Chedotum Kibet Ambrose (deceased)

SECTION TWO

CHALLENGES EXPERIENCED BY FACULTY

CHAPTER SIX

Gender Disparities Among Faculty at Science-Based Programmes in Kenya's Public Universities

Fatuma Daudi

CHAPTER SEVEN

Gender Disparities in Decision Making Levels at Public Universities in Kenya: The Case of Moi University

Walter Kodipo

SECTION THREE

HEALTH RELATED ISSUES

CHAPTER EIGHT

Mothers' Knowledge on Vaccine Preventable Childhood Diseases: A Qualitative Study of Mothers with Children Under Five Years of Age in Uasin Gishu County of Kenya

Theresah Wambui

CHAPTER NINE

Role of Fathers in the Health and Wellness of Their Children

Caroline Sawe

SECTION FOUR

OTHER EDUCATIONAL ISSUES

CHAPTER TEN

Incest: Breaking the Silence on Girls' Issues of Sexuality in Secondary Schools in Kenya

Kamara Margaret Kosgey

CHAPTER ELEVEN

Teacher Preparation Programs in Kenya: The Challenge of Field Placements

Faith Maina

ABOUT THE AUTHORS

Chedotum Kibet Ambrose (deceased) was a lecturer in the Department of Human Resource Management at Moi University before his untimely death. He was also pursuing doctoral studies at Jomo Kenyatta University of Agriculture and Technology (JKUAT).

Fatuma Daudi is lecturer in the Department of Environmental Monitoring Planning and Management at the School of Environmental Studies, University of Eldoret. Fatuma holds a Ph.D in Environmental Planning and Management from Moi University. Her research interests are in Environmental Conservation, Disaster Management and Sustainable Development. Others include Gender, Environment and Community participation. Fatuma has been in the forefront advocating for and helping the girl child and women from marginalized communities through educational access and economic empowerment.

Felicity Wanjiru Githinji is a lecturer at Moi University in Eldoret. She is currently engaged in coordinating, teaching and supervising undergraduate and graduate students. She holds a Ph.D in Sociology of Education, a Master's degree in Sociology of Education and a Bachelor's degree in Special Education (Learning Disabilities) and Home Economics from Kenyatta University. Felicity has taught at different levels of learning including K-12 and community colleges in the USA. She has been a visiting lecturer at the Catholic University of Eastern Africa, Kenyatta University and Africa Nazarene University. Her areas of research include Mentoring and Academic Counselling of students in Higher Education Institutions. She has published a number of articles in international journals and presented at various international conferences.

Kamara Margaret Kosgey is a part-time lecturer at Moi University Eldoret. She holds a Bachelor of Education, a Master's degree in sociology and is pursuing doctoral studies at Moi University. She teaches high school and currently holds the position of Deputy Principal at her school.

Rachel L. Karei is Chair of Hotel and Hospitality Department University of Eldoret. She holds a Bachelor of Science degree in Home Economics from South Carolina State College, MED Home Economics from South Carolina State College and currently pursuing doctoral studies at Moi University. Her research interests include issues pertaining to family life, sexuality and women empowerment

Walter Kodipo is an Administrative Officer at the School of Engineering, Moi University, Eldoret. He holds a Bachelor of Education (Hons) and Master of Arts (History) from Moi University. He is currently pursuing doctoral studies at Moi University. His research interests include peoples' participation in local authority governance, the inclusion of women in governance hierarchies, and gender parities in decision-making organs in public universities in Kenya.

Mary W. Mahugu is a Students Counsellor at Moi University, Eldoret Kenya and Board member of the Moi University HIV/AIDS Control Unit (MUHACU). She holds a Master's degree in Counselling Psychology from Egerton University (2005), Bachelor of Education from Kenyatta University (1990) and a Post-Graduate Diploma in Psychological Counselling from the Kenya Institute of Psychological Counselling (2002). She is currently a doctoral student at Maseno University, Kenya. Her area of specialization is Addictions Counselling with research interests that include alcohol abuse and alcoholism, gender based violence and sexual harassment, among others.

Faith Maina is a professor in the Department of Curriculum and Instruction, State University of New York, Oswego. She has been teaching research methods and educational foundations since 2000. She holds a Ph.D from the University British Columbia, Vancouver, Canada, a Master's degree from Trent University in Ontario, Canada and a Bachelor of Education from Kenyatta University. Her recent accomplishment is the Fulbright award that enabled her to work in Kenya for nine months from September 2011- May 2012.

Caroline Jepkoech Sawe is an administrator at Moi University attached to Academic Division and an IGERD board member representing Academic Division since 2010. She holds a Master's degree in Public Health from Moi University and a Bachelor of Science in Foods Nutrition and Diabetics from Egerton University. She is a part-time lecturer at Moi University in the School of Public

Health and School of Tourism Hospitality and Events Management. Her research interests are in public health nutrition with special focus on children and mothers. Before joining Moi University, she worked at Moi Teaching and Referral Hospital as a nutrition officer. She has also worked as a project coordinator and field nutritionist for an HIV-Nutrition research project in Eldoret Kenya.

Theresah Wambui has a Ph.D in Biomedical Sciences from Linkoping University, Sweden, a Master's degree in Public Health from University of Wales, UK and Diplomas in Nursing, Midwifery and Community Health Nursing from Medical Training College Nairobi. Theresah is currently a Senior Nurse lecturer and the head of Department of Community Health Nursing, Administration and Education at Moi University, Eldoret. Her academic interests include community health with focus on maternal and child health, fertility control and research.

CHAPTER ONE

NURTURING REFLEXIVE PRACTICE: ENGAGING PRO-FESSIONALS IN ACTION RESEARCH PROJECTS

Faith Maina

Many universities around the world hinge promotional and tenure decisions on faculty productivity in terms of knowledge production through research and dissemination. Consequently, the popular adage "publish or perish" is a reality for faculties in many institutions of higher learning. Ideally, institutions of higher learning provide a conducive environment to support faculty in this endeavor given the challenges associated with research, knowledge production and dissemination. To start with, knowledge production is a costly undertaking. It requires time, extensive research, writing skills and adequate resources (Czerniewicz, 2013). Indeed, many universities have research policies which supports faculty to undertake research as part of their workload.

However, this is not always the case especially for institutions of higher learning in Africa. Oanda, Chege and Wesonga (2008) found that there was inadequate funding for research in Kenya's private and public universities and argued that "many deficiencies are not due to lack of capacity but to inadequate research funding" (p. 77). Secondly, Kenya and other developing nations have been the consumers of western methodologies imposed on African universities which in essence does not provide "space to individual voices and paying attention to local realities" (Oanda et al, 2008, p. 77). Needless to say, many African scholars and researchers have therefore pursued knowledge that has little or no relevance to the local realities leading to what (Zambakari, 2011) refers to as "intellectual poverty" and further argues that, "In the field of education a new emphasis on research must be born if the continent is going to pull itself out of the current quagmire" (Par. 6).

As they say, "he who pays the piper picks the tune" is an appropriate metaphor for knowledge production in many African countries (Smith, 2012). Because of lack of an appropriate methodology, knowledge produced is often for consumption in the developed world that pays for the research and has the prestigious academic journals in which they aspire

1

to be published. African scholars therefore become researchers for hire through consultancies in which the name of the scholar may not appear on the publication or they are made to sign a waiver of their rights to the knowledge they have produced (Czerniewicz, 2013). Then there is the issue of low level skills in writing and dissemination. Most universities in the developing world have inadequate training in research skills and methodology. Because more emphasis is focused on teaching for many faculty in Kenya, students pursuing Ph.D or master's degrees are not adequately trained in research methodologies. Indeed, their mentors who are themselves not involved in any research "cannot inspire research" (Oanda et al, 2008, p. 83). Lastly, knowledge production is an isolating affair. People who succeed in knowledge production enjoy an academic community with appropriate training in research skills, mentoring and opportunities for receiving feedback and constructive criticism to their work. There are not many academic professional associations in Kenya to play that role. Hence, many scholars work in isolation without enjoying any kind of mentorship or constructive criticism beyond what they get from their thesis or dissertation committees.

In summary, inadequate research funding, western imposed methodologies, isolation and lack of academic community to mentor and critique are the challenges facing the Kenyan universities where knowledge production is concerned. This project was therefore designed to counter some of these challenges by a) efficient use of resources, b) use of appropriate methodologies and c) development of an academic community.

Efficient use of resources.

Fifteen academic professionals were enrolled in a course titled: "Research, Writing & Dissemination for Academics & Professionals". The course was conducted once a week in the evening for three hours in a central location easily accessible to participants for a period of nine months. These professionals were able to perform their duties and other responsibilities during the time the course was on going. The overarching goal of the course was to equip the professionals with the skills, resources and knowledge needed to conduct and disseminate qualitative research to professional audiences in public forums, preferably conferences, as well as write well developed manuscripts for publication in academic journals. More specifically, the goals included the following:

a) Raise and pursue research questions that address local needs as a way of applying authenticity in knowledge production, relevant for development;

b) Use experiential knowledge and existing studies to develop a conceptual framework;

c) Create a research design that adheres to ethical protocols as laid down by laws protecting human subjects as well as put rigor into the process of data collection;

d) Provide meaning and interpretations to analyzed data;

e) Disseminate to professional as well as general audiences through conferences/workshops and other appropriate venues;

f) Write a full length manuscript and submit to an academic journal (course syllabus, 2011).

Use of appropriate methodologies

The first task for the professionals was to focus on their site of practice and reflect on what was going on. To accomplish this task, they were asked to keep a reflective journal in which they would document what happened in their place of work each day. They were advised to spend at least 10 minutes at the end of the day and answer the following questions: What is happening, what are people doing and what does it mean to them? After repeating this activity for about 10 days, a pattern emerged of the challenges of daily practice in relation to issues highlighted in the course content. Using their experiential knowledge, the professionals were able to identify the challenges they were encountering in their place of work. After analyzing and reanalyzing their experiences with the help of their colleagues, each professional was able to come up with a focus that would lead to the conceptualization of the problem through extensive literature review. Because of the close proximity to individuals who would participate in the study, the professionals elected to use data collection methodologies that sought partnership and collaboration, which is a key tenet of action in research methodology and reflexivity.

Academic Community

The course was run in a seminar format where all professionals were responsible for leading discussions in their area of expertise or raise theoretical and methodological questions espoused in some texts. As such, the professionals honed their skills of sharing their own progress in research but also provided constructive criticism to their peers. Indeed, some of the assignments had to be reviewed by peers before it would be submitted to the instructor. There is no doubt that moving as one cohort for nine months brought the group closer. They mentored each other through constructive feedback and lessened the isolation that characterize the culture of higher learning.

Academic Professionals Engaged in Action Research Project

The purpose of action research is for practitioners to investigate and improve their practice in a process of self-study (Hendricks, 2013). In this process, the knowledge generated is connected to one's practice and the methodology used allows practitioners to create their own theories. The practitioners systematically look at ways to deal with issues they are close to and collaborate with colleagues to find solutions. Rather than choose participants randomly, they work with individuals around whom their everyday work revolve, and data is collected and analyzed for the purpose of informing this practice. Ultimately, the results feedback into the action research cycle so that the study is continuous, flexible and constantly revolving (Hendricks, 2013). It is against this back drop that the authors in this volume developed their studies and the topics which emerged mirrored the work of the professionals which can loosely be divided into four broad categories as follows:

Section 1: Challenges experienced by college students

Section 2: Challenges experienced by faculty

Section 3: Health related issues

Section 4: Other issues in education

SECTION 1: Challenges Experienced by College Students

Chapters in section 1 engage with challenges experienced by students in higher institutions of learning. Rachel Karei had observed a few female students in her classes were pregnant. She knew that these pregnancies were unplanned because the students were in their first year of college. This had happened in spite of the much availed conception control methods at the university clinics, government hospitals/clinics and privately owned hospitals/clinics. There is no doubt that unplanned pregnancies interfere with the students' education and their general social economic welfare. Some students lose their lives in the process of trying to procure abortions and a good number are also infected with sexually transmitted infections including HIV/AIDS. Karei therefore investigated factors leading to unplanned pregnancies by college female students and barriers to the use of conception control. The study utilized qualitative methodologies where several focus group discussions were held with a conveniently sampled group of students. Idleness, too much free time, lack of extracurricular activities, alcohol abuse, ignorance due to lack of proper information on sexuality among others were reasons given for unplanned pregnancies.

Felicity Githinji observed the low performance of female commuter students (FCS) compared to their residential counterparts. Using individual interviews, Focus Group Discussions (FGDs) and analysis of documents, Githinji found that FCS faced challenges that affected their academic performance in institutions of higher learning irrespective of whether they lived with parents, relatives, colleagues or in a hostel outside the campus. Female commuter students in this study had few opportunities to interact with faculty and other students, faced insecurity and sexual harassment from predators such as matatu touts (popular public transportation in Kenya), their male counterparts and some lecturers. They attributed their low performance to having little time to study because of other responsibilities, poverty and financial problems leading to poor housing, prostitution, tardiness and chronic absenteeism.

Mary Mahugu had observed the problem of poor academic performance and social exclusion of college student mothers. By reviewing existing research, Mahugu had found that college student mothers did not perform as well as non-mothers. This clearly indicates that mothers in college face certain challenges that curtail their attainment of good quality college education and the subsequent credentials within the stipulated time span. They include structural barriers in the institution, inadequate social and financial support as well as limited access to academic resources. Mahugu explored ways of eliminating or minimizing these challenges so the student mothers could enjoy their college experience, perform well academically and complete their studies in a timely manner. Using a qualitative methodology, two focus group discussions were organized around two thematic areas: a) challenges faced by the student mothers and how they affect their academic performance, and b) how these challenges can be overcome. Eight purposively selected participants conducted and directed the discussion. Individual interviews were also conducted with six purposefully selected mothers. The study found out that college student mothers are an under-served social group whose social inclusion as a minority group in higher education is long overdue.

Ambrose Kibet Chedotum had observed a high level of examination anxiety among his college students. He therefore decided to investigate the impact of examination anxiety and whether indeed, it led to exam cheating. Recent research has shown that students faced with extreme examination anxiety were prone to cheating. A thirteen item questionnaire was given to fifty (50) college students comprising 10 first years, 9 second years, 10 third years, 10 fourth years and 11 postgraduate students. The study found that sudents with high examination anxiety, panic and while under extreme pressure they are often tempted to cheat. The findings also showed that students have invented newer and cleverer methods of examination cheating. It is clear that effective intervention strategies need to be put in place to reduce (and possibly eliminate) anxiety as a way of lessening examination cheating.

SECTION 2: Challenges Experienced by Faculty

This section of the collection brings chapters that focus on some of the challenges experienced by faculty members. Fatuma Daudi observed the gender disparity among faculty in science-based departments. Daudi therefore sought to find out the causes of the disparity from the experiences of women lecturers in a science-based program. Using in-depth interview and document analysis, she found that a great disparity exists despite the fact that there are many qualified women. There is need to increase the number of women in science-based programs at public universities as a way of bringing diversity and enhancing the quality of such programs.

Walter Kodipo also observed the disparities in gender representation at the decision-making level of the university. By utilizing purposive sampling, 30 female members of the middle level staff population participated in the study. Using an unstructured questionnaire and content analysis of documents obtained from administration offices, the study sought to assess the academic needs of middle level female staff, establish the challenges faced and establish whether there was an academic career development program for female staff to tackle matters of gender disparitoes during promotion at the university. The findings revealed awareness that promotion to higher levels of university governance depends on the efforts made to further education. However, there are no support programs targeting the female middle level staff to increase their education.

SECTION 3: Health Related Issues

Chapters in this section focus on health issues as observed by professionals in the health related fields. Theresah Wambui observed that few mothers understood clearly the process of immunization even though it is one of the most important public health interventions, and cost effective strategy to reduce both morbidity and mortality associated with infectious diseases. Through qualitative methodologies, Wambui explored the mothers' knowledge on vaccine preventable childhood diseases. Seven focus group interviews and two groups of in-depth interviews were carried out with the mothers who had at least one child less than five years old. The study found that most mothers could not define immunization but perceived it to be of great importance because it protects their children from getting infectious diseases that could cause disability and even death. The mothers obtained this information from various sources and were for the most part unaware which childhood diseases could be prevented from immunization. Consequently, some mothers failed to bring their children to the clinic for immunization due to lack of finance, ignorance and sickness. The study revealed that although awareness of the preventable diseases was good, most mothers had their children immunized based on the decisions made by health care givers and recommendations from other people. Clearly, more campaigns to empower mothers with appropriate knowledge and information regarding immunization against preventable childhood diseases need to be urgently implemented.

Caroline Sawe had observed that fathers played a lesser role in the health and well-being of their young children. Influence of father's care on health issues on child development is as great as the influence of mother's care. Recent research had shown that the father's involvement influences the child's cognitive development and functioning. Children with stronger father-figure support felt more competent and socially accepted and had fewer depressive symptoms than those who did not. Using observation and unstructured questionnaires, Sawe found that most fathers agreed that it was important to be involved in their children's health and wellness. However, work commitments, cultural beliefs and norms were the main barriers which hinder that involvement. The study has significant implications for policy makers and recommends introduction of programs that could raise awareness on the importance of fathers' roles in the upbringing of children at all ages.

SECTION 4: Other Educational Issues

The final section focuses on issues outside the academia. Authors were part of the professional group. Kamara Margaret Kosgey had observed a girl in her school emotionally traumatized by an incestuous relationship with a close relative. Incest, defined as an intimate sexual relationship among relatives, is a taboo subject which is rarely discussed or acknowledged in many communities. Anecdotal research shows that many parents and community members still refuse to acknowledge the existence of incest in their communities. Yet the practice exists in some homes with detrimental consequences to victims. Through interviews, content analysis of student essays and focus group discussions with high school students, Kosgey found that incest was a reality and often has a negative impact on students' academic performance. Students narrated horror stories of the vice that sometimes innocently develop early in life, only later to turn into shame, guilt and regret when they grew up. Some of the victims found it hard to abandon the practice even though they were well aware that they would be shunned and ridiculed if their secret came into the open. Other forms of incest involved mature sexual pests like fathers, uncles, cousins and other relatives to whom parents entrust the care of their young girls. These sexual predators were found to force incest through violence, rape, threats, coercion or blackmail, causing trauma, low self-esteem and poor academic performance. Recommendations include enhancing communication of issues relating to girl children through counseling, classroom discussions, school debates, media support, awareness campaigns and teacher/parent involvement.

Faith Maina had observed some problems associated with field placement at a teachers training college. Field placement is an important component of teacher preparation because it allows teacher candidates to apply and reflect on their content, professional and pedagogical knowledge, skills as well as dispositions, in a variety of settings. Maina investigated how teachers in the primary teacher training college were being prepared, specifically in the area of field placement. Data obtained through observations during training practice, reflective journals by student teachers and unstructured questionnaires indicate that field placement was not a valued component even though recent research suggests that it is the single most important element in teacher preparation programs.

Conclusion and Way Forward

Without a doubt, developing countries are severely challenged in terms of knowledge production especially due to lack of funding, use of western imposed methodologies and lack of a vibrant academic community. As demonstrated by these budding scholars, it does not have to always be like this. Innovative ways to increase productivity can be found and if well nurtured, would increase productivity in knowledge production. This is a win-win situation because the dissemination of knowledge produced through publications would bring prestige to the institution while individual scholars would get that elusive promotion.

References

Czerniewicz, L. (2013). Confronting global knowledge production inequities. *University World News: Global Edition Issue No: 287* Retrieved on December 20, 2013. http://www.universityworldnews.com/article.php?story=20130913161503686

Hendricks, C. (2013). Improving Schools with Action Research: A reflective practice approach. New York: Pearson Press.

Oanda, I. O., Chege, F.N & Wesonga, D.M (2008). Research and Knowledge Production in Private Universities and Programs in Kenya. A chapter in Privatization and Private Higher Education in Kenya: Implications for Access, Equity and Knowledge Production. ISBN: 2-86978-218-7; ISBN 13: 978286978218. Retrieved on December 21, 2013 from http://www.codesria.org/IMG/pdf/4-kenya-edu.pdf

Ondari-Okemwa, O. (2011). Knowledge production and distribution by institutions of higher education in sub-Saharan Africa: Opportunities and challenges. South African Journal of Higher Education. Vol. 25(7)

Smith, L. T. (2012). Decolonizing methodologies: Research and Indigenous people.2nd Edition, London & New York: ZED Press.

Zambakari, C. (2011). Africa and the poverty of knowledge production. *Pambazuka,* Vol. 11-3 (556). Retrieved on December 21, 2013 from http://pambazuka.org/en/category/features/77655.

SECTION ONE

CHALLENGES EXPERIENCED BY COLLEGE STUDENTS

CHAPTER 2

UNPLANNED PREGNANCIES AND BARRIERS TO USE OF CONTRACEPTION AMONG COLLEGE FEMALE STUDENTS IN KENYAN PUBLIC UNIVERSITIES

Rachel L. Karei

Unplanned Pregnancies

In my twenty eight years of teaching at university and middle level colleges, I have witnessed many young women dropping out of college or deferring their studies after becoming pregnant. I have seen some students single-handedly raising a child and pursuing their studies, after being abandoned by the man responsible for the pregnancy. The National Campaign (2009), in agreement with this observation, states that these unplanned, and often unwanted pregnancies, result in a large number of single parents who struggle with finances, relationships, and a host of challenging health, educational and social consequences for their children. Trying to balance school work and parenting with limited resources is a big challenge to these young mothers who are also college students.

I have observed devastated parents coming to pick bodies of their daughters who died trying to procure abortions. I have been a member of a disciplinary committee where a young woman was summoned to appear for abandoning a baby somewhere in a bush. When asked why she abandoned her baby, her only defense was "I could not cope with being a student mother. I had no one to turn to for help and I couldn't take it anymore." (Personal communication) My Christian teaching and upbringing put emphasis on sexual abstinence until marriage, but over the years as I taught courses on Human Sexuality at university level I have realized that insisting on abstinence, as the only method of birth control, may not be a practical teaching in this day and age however much it may be the ideal practice. Guidance, counseling and education on safer sex are imperative if unplanned pregnancies are to be reduced among college female students. My concern is why women at the college level in this day and age continue to get unplanned pregnancies when there are readily available conception control methods in the public hospitals and more so in their own college clinics.

Female students I have talked to share that the new found freedom from parents and boarding school matrons make them seek multiple sexual partners once they come to college. When the women later discover that they are pregnant they may not even know the identity of their unborn child's father. Even some known fathers may deny responsibility leaving the young women to struggle on their own. In conversation with some of the victims, they confided that while many of the fathers are college students who were just out to have fun, a good number of them turn out to be married men who eventually deny responsibility. Many of the victims have had to defer their studies to take care of the children.

Barriers to Contraception Use and Risky Sexual Behaviour

In reviewing literature for this study, a number of themes emerged:

a) Policy on pregnancy prevention at college and university levels;
b) College female students at risk of unplanned pregnancies;
c) Impact of unplanned pregnancies and
d) Unprotected sex as a risk factor

Policy on pregnancy prevention at college and university level

Luzer (2009) explains that policy about pregnancy prevention is often concentrated in high schools and the lower levels of learning institutions. This may be due to the fact that policy makers assume that high school and primary students are still minors who need some protection. It is also assumed that at the university/college level people are mature, know how babies are made, and know how to protect themselves from the dangers of unprotected sexual activities and to control their desires (Davis, 1998). Davis (1998) argues that by the time teenagers enter college they think they know about some aspects of sex only to get surprised when they realize that they are naive about other aspects. On one hand, these teenagers also grow up surrounded by glorified sexual images in the media where sex and sexuality is emphasized. On the other hand, they are bombarded with constant warnings from parents and churches that sex is inappropriate and immoral. When these persons get into college, away from the watchful eyes of their parents, they engage in casual sex and all they have been told about sexuality is forgotten (Davis 1998). This is further supported by Tshwane University of Technology (2011), which state that "student pregnancy at tertiary institutions worldwide is increasing every year despite the assumption that students have sufficient knowledge of the risks of unprotected sex".

Another reason pregnancy prevention at the university level may be complicated is the fact that the college women are assumed to be adults since they are 18 years of age or more (Luzer, 2009). College students also think that they have information on pregnancy prevention because of what they learn in high school. However, many of them simply do not remember what they were taught, they have gaps in what they know, harbor inaccurate information or rely on information that is not up to date (the National Campaign 2009). Moreover, many universities have clinics where conception control information is given. Some students use the services provided while others do not, making unplanned pregnancies a reality among college women.

College female students at risk of unplanned pregnancies

Olaitan (2010) suggests that the problem of unwanted pregnancy can be due to poverty, ignorance on the use of contraceptives and general moral laxity. He continues to suggest that parents also do not take time to teach the correct things about sex to their children and the children only get incorrect information on sexuality from friends, books, and television, among other sources. Often, information from these sources is grossly inaccurate and misleading.

According to Hingson, Heeren, Winter & Wechsier (2003) drinking of alcohol to the point of intoxication may increase the likelihood that adolescents and young adults engage in sexual behaviour. This behaviour increases the likelihood of unplanned pregnancies and the incidences of sexually transmitted infections. Ma, et al (2009), a study carried out among university students in China on early indulgence of sexual activity, found out that young people who engaged in sexual activity at an early age were at greater risk of a wide range of sexual and reproductive health problems. The study showed a clear trend indicating that early onset of sexual activity was associated with the increase of Sexually Transmitted Infections (STIs), unplanned pregnancy, induced abortions, multiple sexual partners and reduced condom use. They concluded that early sexual intercourse exposure was a significant predictor of unwanted pregnancies, including abortions and STD/HIV infections. Ma et al (2009) emphasizes that controlling the age of first sex encounter is important in reducing these risks.

Ma et al's findings concur with those of Adhikari (2009) who also found that a good percentage of both male and female students had their first sexual intercourse without their consent and that most

15

of them did not use protection during their first sexual encounter, which also increased the likelihood of an unplanned pregnancy.

Jancin (2011) conducted a study to better understand the phenomenon of unplanned pregnancies in two and four year colleges in the United States. The study identified nine risk factors which include the following:

(i) Girls in a physically abusive relationship were more likely to get pregnant

(ii) Those that have used the emergency pill within the previous year were at risk of having an unplanned pregnancy

(iii) Low achievement in academics, a 'c' grade and below, also increased the likelihood of an unplanned pregnancy

(iv) Those girls that had unprotected sex in the past year as a result of drinking alcohol were also a significant risk factor.

Impact of unplanned pregnancy on female college students

The issue of unplanned pregnancy among college students is hardly ever discussed, yet the majority of today's college students engage in sexual intercourse generally with multiple partners. According to Erenel & Golbas (2010), unplanned pregnancies among youth not only affect their reproduction and sexual health, but also bring about some social problems such as the end of their educational life, or suspension from school for an indefinite period of time. They end up becoming parents at an early age. Most often they end up becoming single parents, get into unstable future relationships with a host of challenging health, educational and social consequences for their children (Erenel & Golbasi, (2010). A study by Moltz (2009) also found that, without question, unplanned pregnancies have a tremendous negative impact on the affected students and their studies. They lose a lot of valuable class time especially those women that juggle between academics and taking care of the child. Olaitan (2010) explains that unwanted pregnancy poses health risks to the mother as well as to the child, such as prematurity, low birth weight, birth injuries and damage that can occur in the birth process. He further argues that some of these victims may also be forced to cohabit with the boy or man responsible for the pregnancy and such forced cohabitation hardly lasts (Olaitan, 2010).

Unprotected sex as a risk factor

Erenel & Golbas (2010) found that the sexual life of young persons who are devoid of basic knowledge of sexuality information, especially about safe sexual behaviour bring about some risks. In a similar study, Murray & Miller (2000) explained that unprotected sexual intercourse contributed towards many of the health and social problems experienced by adolescents and young adults. Unwanted pregnancy and Sexually Transmitted Diseases (STDs) are wide spread and many health professionals consider unplanned pregnancies and STDs a major health concern for college students. Miller and Murray (2000) concluded that it only takes a person to have sex one time to become pregnant or be infected with an STD.

A study done by DePaul (2007) reported that young peoples' reasons for foregoing a condom or some other form of conception control may have to do with the urgency of the moment. This study revealed the possibility that the youth may not so much fear getting pregnant but are more concerned about contracting Sexually Transmitted Infections (STIs). Young people are more alarmed by the prospects of contracting an STD than an unplanned pregnancy. They think that having an STD is much worse than an unplanned pregnancy. Korra & Haile (1999) reports that adolescents in many developing countries of Africa, Asia, and Latin America have little information about sex and reproduction, putting themselves at considerable risk of unwanted pregnancy.

According to Noone & Young (2010) adolescence is a vulnerable time when unwise choices on sexual activities can have lasting consequences. Parental and child communication can assist adolescents with pregnancy prevention. The study showed that teens viewed parents as an important influence on their sexual decision making, however many of them reported never having such conversations regarding sex with their parents. They identified mothers as a strong support for information and sometimes access to contraceptive. The teens in this study reported that parents are the biggest influence in their decision-making about sex. However, teens reported that no one ever talked to them about sex. He also found out that a lot of teens just desired to hear their parent tell them to wait or not to have sex.

The purpose of this study was therefore to investigate why college students continue to be victims of unplanned pregnancy even with all the available information and contraception availed to them.

Methodology

The study utilized a qualitative approach targeting students from a large public university. It was carried out within a constituent college that has a population of more than 6000 students taking degree and diploma courses.

Sample population

Convenience sampling method was used to get students willing to participate in the study. A total of 27 female students agreed to participate. Of the 27, 15 were in a degree program ranging from year 1 to 4. 12 female students were from the diploma program in their 1st and 2nd year of study.

Instruments

Focus group discussion (FGD) was the main instrument used in the study. An interview guide with a number of questions directed the discussions. This helped to pursue the same line of inquiry and manage the FGDs in a more systematic and comprehensive way. Students taking degree courses formed one group and those taking diploma courses formed another group. Two FGDs were held for every group making a total of four FGDs. Two meetings for each group was necessary to make sure each participant had an opportunity to give her views. Those students pursuing a degree were grouped separately from those pursuing a diploma as a precaution against intimidation.

Procedure

I explained to the female students in both my degree and diploma classes the objectives of the study and encouraged them to invite their friends who were in other schools and or departments for a FGD meeting. I gave them specific dates when the FGD would take place as well as the venue. I had reserved one of a large laboratory class room where we could sit around forming a circular arrangement. The female students who showed up for the FGD were requested to sign a letter of consent that explained their rights. They could withdraw from the study any time without penalty and their participation was strictly voluntary confidential. All of them agreed and signed a letter of consent and allowed for the discussions to be audio-taped. After the first FGD we all realized that we had not exhausted all the questions and there were girls that did not get a chance to either react or give their opinion. As a group we felt that there was a need to meet again the following week same time and at the same place. Unlike the first FGD the second time all of the girls for the two groups were on time.

Findings

The purpose of the study was to establish factors leading to unplanned pregnancies and barriers to the use of conception control methods among college female students in Kenyan public universities. A number of factors emerged, which will be discussed under the following themes:

a) Early lessons on menstruation;
b) Sexual activity and conception control;
c) Services offered at the University for sexuality information and conception control method;
d) Reasons girls get pregnant at the college and
e) Unprotected sex, unplanned pregnancies and sexually transmitted infections.

Among the students who participated in the FGD were three girls who were victims of unplanned pregnancies. This factor was, however, not a consideration in the sampling process they just volunteered to participate in the study. These girls gave their contributions not as victims and were not at any point used as references. Eight of the participants were first years and therefore were only two and a half months old in the university at the time of the study.

Early lessons on menstruation

When the girls were asked the source of their prior knowledge about sexuality and menstruation, only a small number of girls admitted that they got the information from their mothers. The majority of the girls, especially those that entered boarding schools in the primary and secondary education period, got sexuality related information from older girls. Their schools would organize social meetings where older girls would pass on what they knew or remembered to the younger girls. The information would be scant and watered down in that the older girls would only pass on what they could remember from what had been previously passed on by others. Older girls would only tell what was passed on to them by those ahead of them. This mostly touched on what to do when they started their menstrual cycle, what to expect and how to dress up. If the older girls had the wrong information from those that were ahead of them then the same wrong information would be passed on to the younger girls. A few girls reported that they got the information from their churches where guest speakers would be invited to speak to the youth on selected topics. These forums would educate them on their bodies and the changes that take place as they matured. This was a lucky group in that experts on the topic of sexuality were their guest speakers and so gave them the correct information. The majority of the girls wished that their mothers talked to them concerning sex and sexuality. This was well summarized by one girl who shared thus:

> When I told my mother that I had started menstruating, she made a point of always rebuking me in my mother tongue telling me, "Don't get close to the boys or you get pregnant. If you get close to the boys, you will never see your periods again and when you don't see your periods it means you are pregnant." For a long time I was scared of being close to the boys because no one explained to me what it meant to be close to the boys. I could not ask my mother what she actually meant by being 'close to the boys' so I stayed away from the boys. When I went to high school a group of people from Proctor and Gamble came to our school and taught us about our bodies and how babies are made and that is when I relaxed about boys otherwise for a long time I was very scared of getting close to boys. My mum should have explained to me what she meant by being close to a boy, I was scared to ask and I guess she was embarrassed to explain.

Many girls confessed that whereas older girls in their schools had talked to them about menstruation and what to expect, the information did not quite prepare them and their first experience was very scaring. Two girls shared the following:

> I don't think I had all the information to prepare me for it. The older girls only used their own experiences to teach us which were not much.

> For me I thought it was a one day experience. After the second day I was scared and thought I had a bad illness, I did not expect it to go on for more than a day. No one prepared me for that. My own mother did not even tell me how long it would take. When I told her that my periods were still on the second day she just told me not to worry it will stop. Each day for me was a nightmare as I waited for it to stop.

Another girl however had a different experience expressed thus:

I was excited because most of the girls in my class already had seen their periods. I was a bit behind. Every time they talked about their experiences they would whisper so I didn't get to know what they were saying, they kept referring to me as a child. When I finally got my periods I could not wait to let them know I was also a mature woman. I, however, did not know that it was not a one day experience. I was excited that I was finally a mature woman but scared that it might go on forever.

Sexual activity and conception control

The study revealed that girls got information on sexual activity and conception control from a number of sources. These include talking to peers, reading books, from their mothers (asking them to stay away from the boys) or in the human sexuality class taught at the university. Some girls revealed that they had to piece up information obtained from several sources to try and make sense of what sexual activities was all about. Two of the girls said that their mothers explained to them in detail what it was all about and what they needed to do to keep the boys away.

My mum was quite frank with us. She taught me and my younger brother and she touched on very intimate things to the point that I felt embarrassed on her behalf and wondered why she would talk to us like that even in the presence of my younger brother. I later realized that the information she imparted on us was quite helpful. Without it, I would have made very major mistakes.

Another girl who first heard about sexual activity from peers had this to say:

When I went to high school there was this big girl who had a figure 8 (or hour glass figure) and she made a point of telling all of us that if we desired to have a figure like hers we had to drink sperms mixed with eggs. That scared many of us but we also desired a figure like hers. We always wondered where to get the sperms mixed with eggs and I know if I got them I would have drunk it. I am so glad I never got to drink it because later I got to know that she was misleading us and actually encouraging us to be sexually active and the actual drinking of eggs mixed with sperms was not real.

Services and information given at the university on sexuality and conception control

The girls expressed the desire for better services and people that will give them needed information without judging or condemning them. The girls felt that, whereas the personnel at the university clinic were well trained, they were not providing appropriate information as one participant shared:

> When you go to them (staff at the clinic) they give you a very disapproving look that scares you. They need to employ younger people that we can talk to and who understand our "sheng" (communication language of the Kenyan youth). Many of the people working there are old enough to be our parents. When you go to somebody who gives you a motherly or fatherly look, you end up forgetting what you wanted or just pretend that you went there for some other reason.

Reasons girls get pregnant at the college

The girls gave a laundry list of why college students become pregnant including the following:

- **Idleness**: According to the students there is so much idle time and therefore students spend their time dating and having sex. There are not many extracurricular activities to fill their time; sports are not emphasized even though college students had a lot of stored energy and they therefore used that energy for having sex.

- **Financial needs**: A number of girls come from humble back grounds; they do not get enough money from home for their needs. They end up prostituting themselves to make ends meet. One girl had this to say, "Prostitution at the university is the order of the day. People to buy the commodity are there. It is a willing seller willing buyer kind of thing".

- **Peer pressure**: One participant had this to say:
  > The element of post modernity, everyone is doing it. No one wants to be left out or be the odd one out. Peer pressure is also there. Pressure from the boyfriend, "If you love me you have to show me by having sex with me". If you refuse, you lose him and he will get a girl who will sleep with him, so to keep him you give in. Girl friends will also pressure you into doing it. If you associate with girls who do it you will end up doing it also.

- **Lack of parental supervision**: One participant had this to say while the others were in agreement.

> Too much freedom! No rules! The up to ten o'clock rule does not work [dorms are locked up at 10pm]. Many people do it before ten. There are no parents and no matrons watching over you. Many people just do it willingly and readily. People also have sex during the day so some rules are not worth having.

Unprotected sex, unplanned pregnancies and sexually transmitted infections

The study revealed that many of the girls get pregnant due to carelessness, ignorance and lack of adequate information. Students feared being seen buying condoms or other forms of conception control as shared by one participant, "When they see you going for any conception control method, people think you are promiscuous and many girls want to give the impression they have 'chilled'. Many girls are afraid of being thought of as immoral and some girls are also afraid of using conception control methods because they do not have information on the side effects. While there is so much advertisement in the media on the use of condoms and other methods, the information is scant and not much is explained as to whether there are side effects or not. There are many myths on the use of conception control methods. One advert, for example, only shows several people who supposedly had sex without any form of protection. One end up "screaming no", the other one hits some kind of "tragedy" and that ends the commercial with no further explanation. Lack of proper information leaves the girls compromised. They are scared of the consequences as one participant shared

> There was this girl who was told that when you use a condom your legs at the thighs will start swelling. The girl believed and would not be persuaded to use a condom because she totally believed that her legs will swell. A lot of girls even at the college level still believe in myths and old wives tales.

Participants revealed that many girls abuse drugs and alcohol. When drunk they engage in unprotected sex sometimes with multiple partners. There was also the issue of girls wanting to win the trust and love of their partners as shared by a girl who said: "Having unprotected sex is an ultimate status symbol showing my man that I trust him and he can also trust me and that we are one".

Ways to reduce cases of unwanted pregnancy

Participants gave suggestions of how cases of unwanted pregnancies can be reduced at the university. They suggested that correct information should be given to the students at the right time. The students that were fortunate to take the Human Sexuality course offered in my department had this to say:

> The human sexuality course is very helpful in that it gives the right information that opens up one's mind and guards against many myths. The fact that it is taught in the first semester of first year and to both boys and girls helps us to understand the ways our different bodies work and learn how to control our emotions instead of giving in to the "id" that wants to get in now.

There was a feeling among students that there is too much free time. Students suggested that lecturers ensure students are well occupied to reduce idle time. Games and other sports should be made compulsory so that students can spend their energies on such other activities. The clinical staff should be more discreet and information given at the clinic be confidential. There was a feeling among students that information they give at the clinic can be accessed by anyone. Conception control methods should be availed in discreet places not in the open and that they should not be asked many personal questions. The clinical staff should endeavor to be gentle, understanding and friendly.

Discussion and Conclusions

The purpose of this study was to identify the causes of unplanned pregnancies among university college female students. Collected data revealed that while some parents and some schools have tried to educate the girls on changes that take place as they mature, the information and sources of information given are inadequate. The data indicated the need for parents to give correct information on sexuality and avoid misleading phrases like 'if you get near a boy you will get pregnant'. Such phrases only confuse the youth especially the girls. The study also revealed that alcohol abuse, lack of proper information, idleness, peer pressure, poverty and ignorance are among the major causes of unplanned pregnancies. Unfriendly staff at the clinics, questions asked at the clinic and by the clinical staff who are old enough to be their parents embarrass students especially the female students. This hinders them from seeking the needed information and help.

This study took place over a period of two weeks. In the two weeks I met with each group twice for about one hour making a total of four hours for each group. This may not have been sufficient time for a proper FGD. The use of convenient sampling may also have created some kind of bias in that only those that were available were given a chance to give their views. All students did not have an equal chance of being part of the FGD and the male voice was not given a chance to be heard. However, even with these limitations the study produced significant findings.

According to the participants, alcohol abuse was one of the factors that strongly came out as the cause for unplanned pregnancies. When the girls get drunk they are likely to have unprotected sex that may lead to unplanned pregnancies. This is consistent with Hingson et al (2003) & Jancin (2011) where they state that, drinking alcohol to the point of intoxication increases the likelihood of unprotected sexual activities that may result in unplanned pregnancies and sexually transmitted infections. Girls in this study also reported that lack of proper information on sexuality was a contributor to unplanned pregnancies. Parents and schools did not empower them with the necessary information on sexuality. Being told not to get near boys only confused and scared them. This is in agreement with Ernel & Golbas (2010) study that argued that sexual life of young persons with limited basic knowledge of safe sexual behaviour put them at risk of unplanned pregnancies.

It is interesting to note that idleness was identified as a reason why college students engage in sexual activity leading to unplanned pregnancy. This could possibly be that many instructors shy away from giving too much outside of class work for fear that they will be unable to grade or provide adequate feedback. The college could also be unable to provide facilities for individual studies making the students overly reliant on classroom instruction. It could also be possible that facilities for extracurricular activities like sports are not available and students had no avenues to expend their pent up energies.

Another interesting but sad finding was that female students engage in sexual activities as an income generating venture. Some students come from humble backgrounds and the desire to want to live like everyone else or to supplement what they get from parents make them join the oldest trade in the world "prostitution". Other girls prostitute to get money for buying the fine things of life. Even at the college level some girls still believe in myths regarding contraception. A good example was given of the girl who would not be persuaded to use conception control because she believed that using condoms would make her legs swell at the thighs. It is also mind boggling at this age and time that female college students would think that having unprotected sex was an ultimate 'status symbol".

Implications for the study

It is clear from this study that extracurricular activities like sports and other activities should be made mandatory to help students become active and use their energies in more constructive ways. This calls for a more systematic development of university curriculum that puts more demands on the student. College instructors should be encouraged to integrate their curriculum with research activities that enable students to do individual studies. This would only be possible if instructors are provided adequate professional development and libraries are equipped with the necessary resources.

There was also a suggestion that information on conception control be availed at the clinic discreetly. Many students are embarrased of being seen going for contraceptives. Girls want to give the impression they have "chilled", slang for not sexually active. Clinical staff at the conception control unit should be more open and non-judgmental. It would even help a little if younger people were hired to take care of the students. Girls in this study felt that a person closer to their age would understand them better and understand their mode of communication. Such a person should be able to dialogue without being judgmental to ease the tension. They felt that having to deal with an older person at the clinic was just like having one of their parents there. "It is just like talking to your father or mother", one student said. Another one added, "The staff at the clinic give you that disapproving look and you leave there feeling condemned and guilty".

Most of the students in the study felt that there is an urgent need to introduce the human sexuality course to all students in their first year of study of university or college. This will help them get the proper information before they get into trouble. The students that had taken the course felt that the information given was quite helpful. According to the students it fills many gaps and help clear many cultural beliefs and myths. Further studies are needed using a larger sample or even a longitudinal study that would track the behaviour of students who directly enroll in a human sexuality course at first year and the outcome as they exit college in comparison with those who did not enroll. More in depth study with individual interviews over a longer period of time could also provide more insights.

References

Adhikari, R. (2009). Factors Affecting Awareness of Emergency Contraception Among College Students in Kathmandu, Nepal BCM *Women's Health,* 9(27) doi: 10.1186/1472-6874-9-27

Davis, S. (1998). Birth Control Basics- Sex on Campus. From http:findarticle.com/p/articles/mi_m1608/is_n9_v14/ ai_21099911/ retrieved on 10/21/2011

DePaul, A. (2007). Unintended pregnancy down among teens but up for young adults: why an increasing number of 20-somethings are rolling the dice and getting pregnant. AlterNet. Retrieved from http://www.alternet.org/story/62429/unintended_pregnancy_ down_among_teens_but_up_for_young_adults on 10/20/2011

Erenel, A. S. & Golbasi, Z. (2010) Unprotected Sexual Intercourse and Unplanned Pregnancy Experience of Turkish University Students Springer *Science+ Business, LLC2010*

Hingson, R., Hereen, T., Winter, M. R., & Wechsler, H. (2003). Early age of first drunkenness as a factor in college student unplanned and unprotected sex attributed to drinking. *Pediatrics.* 111(1):34-41.

Jancin, B. (2011). Evaluating unintended pregnancy in unmarried female students retrieved on 10/20/2011 from http://www.internationalmedicinenews.com/news/women-s-health-article/evaluating

Korra, Anteneh and Mesfin Haile. 1999. Sexual behaviours and level of awareness on reproductive health among youths: Evidence from Harar, Eastern Ethiopia. *Ethiopian Journal of Health Development* 13(2): 107-113.

Luzer, D. (2009). Pregnant college students. *Washington Monthly.* Retrieved from http://www.washingtonmonthly.com/college_guide/ blog/pregnant_college_students.php on 10/21/2011

Ma, Q., Kihara, M.o., Cong, L., Xu, G., Pan, X., Zamani, S., Ravari, S. M., Zhang, D., Homma, T. & Kihara, M. (2009). Early initiation of sexual activity: a risk for sexuality transmitted diseases, HIV infection, and unwanted pregnancy among university students in China. BMC *Public Health2009, 9:111 doi: 10.1186/1471-2458-9-111* or http//www.biomedcentral.com/1471-2458/9/11

Moltz, D. (2009). A Different kind of pregnant student. *Inside Higher Ed.* Retrieved from http://www.insidehighered.com/news/2009/11/25/pregnancy on 10/20/2011

Murray,S.R. & Miller, J.L. (2000) Birth control and condom usage among college students *CAHPERD Journal,* 25 (1)

Noone, J. & Young, H. M. (2011). Rural mothers experiences and perceptions of their role in pregnancy prevention for their adolescent daughters from *JOGNN,39, 27-36; 20110.doi: 10.1111/j.1552-6909.01082.x* or http://jognn.awhonn.org

Olaitan, O. L. (2010) Perception of university students on unwanted pregnancy in south west Nigeria. *American Journal of Social and Management Sciences* ISSN Print: 2156-1540, ISSN Online:2151-2151,doi;10.5251/ajsms.2010.1.2.196.200

The National Campaign to Prevent Teen and Unplanned Pregnancy (2009). Unplanned Pregnancy and Community Colleges. Retrieved from http://www.thenationalcampaign.org/ on 12/11/2012

Tshwane University of Technology (2011). Student pregnancy increase drastically. Retrieved from http://www.tut.ac.za/News/Pages/pregnancies.aspx on 15/11/2012

CHAPTER 3

CHALLENGES AFFECTING THE ACADEMIC PERFORMANCE OF COLLEGE FEMALE COMMUTER STUDENTS

Felicity Wanjiru Githinji

Introduction and Background

My personal experience as a female commuter student (FCS) during my years as an undergraduate student prompted me to conduct a study on challenges affecting the academic performance of FCS in institutions of higher learning. I had a very hard time balancing studies and other family duties. As a lecturer in a public university, which admits students of different age-groups, programs and modes of study, including regular day time and evening classes, as well school-based classes during the school holidays, it was necessary to investigate systematically the challenges these students experience in the course of their studies. This information is significant in terms of program planning/design as well as intervention strategies that the administration can put into place to mitigate the challenges. The voice of students would also be incorporated into the planning as they get assistance to complete their studies successfully.

The student body range from those pursuing doctoral studies, masters' degrees, undergraduates, and post graduate diplomas in various disciplines. The college campus does not have student hostels and therefore, all students operate as commuters. Some of the students rent rooms in privately owned hostels near campus depending on affordability while others live with their families or guardians. Some students cook in the hostels, while others buy food in nearby restaurants and kiosks. The assumption was that most FCS might have multiple roles and responsibilities. There was no doubt that these students encountered challenges that affected their academic performance. A fundamental goal of studying this population was to to investigate how FCS can improve their academic performance as they pursue their career goals. This would provide some practical solutions that can be used by universities to improve on the academic performance of FCS. Most importantly, to find out what can be done to reduce or eliminate those challenges that continue to plague this population.

Despite residing off-campus, FCS have high academic aspirations and a strong commitment to learning. Several studies comparing FCS and university-owned hostel students suggest that living on campus fosters academic performance through expanded opportunities for integration into the academic (e.g. interaction with faculty) and social systems (e.g. frequency of peer conversations, informal social activities) of college. The stereotypical view is that commuters were less committed to academic pursuits compared with their counterparts who go away to college and live on campus (Jacoby, 2000a; National Resource Centre [NRC], 2001). They are distracted by too many competing demands on their time because of studies/work or family commitments and as a result they are not as involved on campus activities as other students. This is problematic because what students gain from their college experience depends a lot on how much time and effort they put into their studies and other educationally purposeful activities (Pascarella, 2001). The focus of this study therefore, was to find out challenges affecting the academic performance and quality of life of FCS in the institution with the aim of helping them to navigate their campus life successfully and graduate on time.

Challenges Faced by Commuter Students on Academic Performance

Commuter students encounter many challenges that residential students do not (Horn & Berktold, 1998). Research concerning challenges faced by FCS in the universities is abundant (Jacoby, 2000). In the 1980s, the non-traditional student became the norm in student populations in colleges and universities in the western countries (Villella, & Hu, 1991). Non-traditional students are defined as students who are 25 years of age or older, attend colleges on a part-time basis, or commute to school, or any combination of these characteristics. The growth rate of students over 25 years from 1970 to 1985 was 114% compared to a 15% increase in the number of younger students in the University of Chicago (Villella & Hu, 1991). Part-time students have increased from 87% compared to a 22% increase of full-time students. Indeed, 80% of all students attending higher educational institutions are commuters in the developed world (Villella & Hu, 1991).

According to Horn & Berktold (1998), approximately 86% of college and university students in the developed countries were defined as commuter students, that is, students not living in university-owned housing. Jacoby (2000) defined commuters as those students whose place of residence while attending college was not in a campus residence hall or in a fraternity or sorority house. Typically commuter students walked, rode bikes, took public transportation, or drove to campus to go to classes. They often attended classes and then went home or to work, rarely spending additional time outside of the classroom on campus (Horn & Berktold, 1998).

Students commute to campus for several reasons. Unlike many full-time residential students commuter students might have competing responsibilities outside the academic classroom such as family, home, and work interests. For those students who were working full-time, raising a family, or caring for an elderly parent, campus residency was not a viable option (George, Kuh, Robert, Gonyea & Megan, 2001). Also, commuting might have been economically beneficial because many commuter students could not afford to live on campus. Commuting students, as a group, seem to be at a particular risk for attrition because there was less commitment to the institution and re-enrolling was more disruptive to their lives (Noel, 1985).

In reviewing literature for this study, a few themes emerged:
a) little interaction with other students;
b) little interaction with faculty members;
c) transportation Issues and
d) low engagement in social and academic activities.

Little interaction with other students

Commuter students, particularly those in their first-year of study, often have a difficult time "fitting in" to the campus community (Anderson, 1988). Commuter students often find the task of meeting their peers challenging because their only point of contact with other students is in the classroom, a small part of the total college experience (Horn, and Berktold, 1998). Residential students live, eat, study, and socialize together in halls of residence, thus having greater opportunities to make friends and to become socially integrated into the campus community. A great amount of socialization for college students also occurs in the cafeteria, student centre, recreation centre, through extracurricular activities, or during late-night study sessions (Anderson, 1988). Astin, (1993) argues that this peer

31

group interaction positively affects critical thinking skills, cultural awareness, leadership development, and academic development. As a result of not living in residence halls or spending a substantial amount of time on campus, commuter students miss out on these opportunities to "connect" to the university and other students and to enhance their learning and development (Astin, 1993).

Little interaction with faculty members

Pascarella (1993) found that student commuters often face limited contact opportunities with faculty and staff members. They must make additional trips to campus to meet with faculty members during their designated office hours. Unlike residential students, commuter students rarely have the opportunity to observe faculty and staff members on campus involved in non-classroom activities, such as playing sports in the recreation centre or interacting with students in the student centre. According to Pascarella and Terenzini's (1991), these informal student-faculty interactions have been linked to academic performance and to personal and intellectual development for students. The interaction time for commuters with faculty members is often limited to a few minutes between classes or briefly during office hours, leaving commuter students feeling disconnected from the academic system of the university. Commuters often find forming relationships with faculty and administrators difficult because of these limited interactions outside of the classroom due to the fact that they have classes other to attend, while lecturers have to teach other classes.

Tinto (1987) argues that students who have high interaction with their university's academic and social systems are more likely to persist in college. Tinto (1987) further argues that commuter students have lower retention rates than those living on campus. This is because commuter students spend limited time on campus and have limited time creating relationships with other students, faculty, and staff. Therefore, they are less likely to make a strong commitment to the university or its programs and are more likely to drop out of college than residential students (Anderson, 1988).

Transportation issues

According to Horn & Berktold (1998), transportation issues are   major concerns for commuter students. First, commuters often readjust their course schedules to attend classes in large blocks of time, again reducing the hours spent on campus outside of the classroom and the opportunity to become socially and academically integrated into the college community. Some classes may be scheduled at difficult times for commuters to attend, such as early morning or midafternoon. Because of long commutes to school, these students may encounter difficulty attending such classes, which are easily accessible for residential students. Because of the short amount of time spent on campus each day, commuter students have a limited knowledge of the university itself, including the location of buildings, functions of university departments, campus policies and procedures, and current events (Anderson, 1988).

Residential students on the other hand become familiar with the university by spending a substantial amount of time on campus, taking part in student forums, and discussing current campus events in the residence hall or in small groups. Therefore, residential students often have a better understanding of the status of the university, unlike commuter students who must wait to receive pertinent information through mailings or newspaper articles. In addition, greater proximity gives residential students more frequent occasions to establish personal relationships with faculty and staff, who serve as resources and mentors. These mentors may provide assistance and information regarding new policies and procedures (Pascarella, 1993).

Low engagement in social and academic activities

The factors that affect the commuter student's participation and persistence in college are many and varied. These include communications about the educational programs, previous educational success, and the availability of noncredit courses for people with low ability or lack of educational preparedness. Villella and Hu (1991) revealed that the time constraints of college terms and the amount of academic rigor required in college courses can lead to student stress and dissatisfaction. These factors can result in commuter students leaving college (Gleazer, 1980).

It is true that students who live on campus are more engaged overall compared with students who commute. In addition, it appears that the further away from campus (walking distance, driving distance) the less likely a student is to take advantage of the educational resources the institution provides. Thus, proximity to campus makes a difference in commuter students' level of engagement. While a lot of research has been done affecting commuter students in western countries, little is known about commuter students in Kenyan universities and more so, the added challenge of the female commuter student. This study sought to investigate the challenges faced by college female commuter students in large Kenyan institution of higher learning .

Methodology

Research Approach

The study used a qualitative approach. A case study technique was adopted to enable the researcher to achieve, among other things, an in-depth collection and analysis of data from a single case with a variety of backgrounds. According to Cochran (1997), qualitative approach enables a researcher to investigate and describe the current phenomena on focus. The approach was appropriate because it enabled the researcher to describe situations, perceptions, opinions, attitudes and general demographic information that are currently affecting the FCS in the universities. The justification being that issues of female commuter or individual opinions would best be captured through this approach. The method also allowed the researcher to formulate open-ended questions through which a wide and deeper range of responses were sought. Document analysis was applied in instances such as presenting enrolment number of FCS and academic performance.

Study Location

The study was conducted at a constituent college of a large public university. This was among the first established campus, largest and densely populated with a variety of programs and courses of different modes of study, including school-based, regular and evening students, with both undergraduate and masters' degree programmes. It is situated in a mid-sized town and therefore, most of the FCS might have come for their studies in the campus from the rural areas to stay with their spouses/relatives or rented hostels. Hence, the experiences of the FCS in this case may be similar to other campuses that have proximity to large towns.

Target Population

The researcher sampled 16 FCS from first to fourth year of study. Convenience sampling was used to include FCS who came to campus by public means. Female commuter students who walked or drove to campus were not included in the study because they might not have been experiencing any problem by staying near the campus. Those who drove to the campus might not have been experiencing as much hustle as those using public means. The FCS using public transportation would yield deeper insights regarding their perceptions as they board the public means from different stages.

In carrying out the study various factors were to be considered, vis-a-vi FCS who lived with their parents, FCS who lived in off-campus apartments, FCS married with children and living with husbands, and FCS single with children. This would bring out similarities and differences in the challenges faced by FCS in the different environments.

Schematic Representation of Sampled Female Commuter Students

West Campus FCS

One FCS from each Year of Study (First –fourth Year)

FCS who lived with their parents	FCS who lived in off-campus apartments	FCS married with children and living with the husband	FCS Single with children

Instruments for Data Collection

Focus Group Discussions (FGD) for FCS

Focus group discussions were based on the principle of small group dynamics. Krueger (1988) describes the focus group as a special type of group in terms of purpose, size, composition, and procedures. A focus group is typically composed of seven to twelve participants who are unfamiliar with each other and conducted by a trained interviewer. These participants are selected because they have certain characteristics in common that relate to the topic of the focus group. The researcher creates a permissive environment in the focus group that nurtures different perceptions and points of view, without pressuring participants to vote, plan, or reach consensus. The group discussion is conducted several times with similar types of participants to identify trends and patterns in perceptions. Careful and systematic analysis of the discussions provides clues and insights as to how a product, service, or opportunity is perceived. A focus group can also be defined as a carefully planned discussion designed to obtain perceptions on a defined area of interest in a permissive, nonthreatening environment. It is conducted with approximately seven to twelve people by a skilled interviewer. The discussion is relaxed, comfortable, and often enjoyable for participants as they

35

share their ideas and perceptions. Group members influence each other by responding to ideas and comments in the discussion.

FGDs are used to generate information from a "natural" group that usually meets for a common purpose or represents the interests of different collectivises (Oanda 2002). The purpose of keeping the group small is to ensure that all members participate actively in the discussions and all general topics of interest are covered.

The researcher organized convenient time to meet them for the FGD.

Procedure

A week prior to inviting the students to participate in the study, permission was granted by the Dean of the school as well as the coordinator of the programme. Before participating in the interview, each student was requested to sign a consent form. They were informed that participation in the study was voluntary and they could withdraw from the study at any time without penalty. They were also told that what they said was confidential and reported data would not reveal their identity.

Results

In reviewing the data generated by the female commuter students, a number of challenges are observed:

a) Insecurity and sexual harassment from predators (*matatu* touts, lecturers, etc.);

b) Few opportunities to interact with faculty (commute time, over-protective parents/guardians);

c) Few opportunities to interact with other students (commute time, over-protective parents/guardians)

d) Low Academic Performance;

e) Lack of adequate facilities including (classrooms, library, hostels, badly ventilated rooms) and

f) Poverty/ financial problems (poor housing, prostitution, missing classes, tardiness, lack of fare).

Insecurity and sexual harassment from predators

Commuter students reported discomfort in using public means to get to campus. They were often harassed by *matatu* touts who called them *maresh-warembo*. This sentiment was well summarized by a student who said: "*Matatu* drivers and conductors seduce us especially when they know that you are a student. They take advantage seeing you as 'immoral' because of the views that campus students are easy to get especially when you offer them money". They also reported that sometimes the means of transport is a problem because the fare is sometimes hiked without notice or the *matatus* may go on strike. This brought about a lot of anxiety for the female commuter students because they were often unsure of whether they will be able to get to college.

Other students reported fear in approaching their male professors as one participant shared thus: "My nature of being a female student limits me to interact with male lecturers because some will take advantage of the closeness and some students will start mocking you saying you are sleeping with the professors to attain [good]marks."

Few Opportunities to Interact with Faculty (commute time, over-protective parents/ guardians)

Although some participants agreed with this, the commute distance did affect their interaction with lecturers. The majority of the participants said that they met lecturers during the lecture hours or after the lectures. One participant said: "I rarely get time to interact [with a lecturer] since I am always in a hurry to get home by public means, and my aunt is too inquisitive about my whereabouts and who I associate with". Another added: "I rarely interact with the lecturers because I need to catch up with buses since they are not many". Another one said "I find it difficult since while the lectures are over, one has to hurry from one class to another."

Few Opportunities to Interact with Other Students (commute time, over-protective parents/ guardians)

Some participants reported that, "We mostly interact with other students occasionally and even meet in their houses". Another participant said, "We interact with other students because we walk home with most of them". Another participant who lived with the parents said: "It was hard to interact because there was no time since they had to hurry back home 'as my parents asked me why I am late." Another one said, "There is no time to interact due to insecurity when going back home late in the evening". One participant said, "With the students it is difficult to get to know most of them because of the little time available." A participant who lived with an aunt said the following;

There was overprotection by my auntie, depriving me the chance to interact with my fellow students or, even have enough time to engage in discussion groups. I also do not have chances to engage in discussion with my colleagues because I arrive to class late and miss part of the lecture.

Low academic performance

One participant shared that, she was not satisfied with her academic performance. She felt that in some subjects she would fail yet she wrote things that she knew were right. Another indicated that, "Some lecturers do not mark examinations fairly because sometimes they were confident yet in the end they ended up failing." They attributed this lack of success in their academic performance to the fact that lecturers set examinations from areas they had not taught or as one participant said:

> I remember the time I sat for my first year examinations I worked so hard in my studies hoping for the best at the end. Ironically what I saw in my provisional transcripts did not please me at all and I believed the marking was unfair and I felt discouraged.

Others indicated that they have not exerted themselves well enough as shared by one participant:

> feel I can do much better. I have not unleashed all my potential, I am not satisfied enough but I hope for better improvement, it is has been difficult to attain the grades that are desired, I am not satisfied because the subjects that I feel I am not well conversant with fail me during examinations and I fail to understand why.

Another participant shared thus, "Some lecturers refuse to repeat themselves in lectures when asked to do so, they tell students to ask their friends or neighbours. Some lecturers were not audible enough or were not serious with their work."

Lack of Adequate Facilities Including (classrooms, library, hostels, badly ventilated rooms)

One participant said, "I cannot be able to use facilities like the library, because sometimes I encounter new things which we are not taught." Another one said, "Because we are crowded, yet facilities are not enough to accommodate us all and so for example, if hostels were located in the campus at least we could easily access". Another FCS said , "Due to large number of students when I sit at the back I do not hear the lecturer, I do not have enough time to study, travelling from home to school is time consuming."

Poverty/ financial problems (poor housing, prostitution, missing classes, tardiness, lack of fare etc.)

Financial problems were some of the challenges cited by the participants. Those who lived on their own often live in poorly constructed and congested houses. This kind of housing is not conducive to studying because of noise pollution or just overcrowding.

Discussion and Conclusion

The purpose of this study was to investigate the challenges faced by FCS in public institutions of higher learning. It is clear that FCS do face challenges such as insecurity and sexual harassment from predators (*matatu* touts, lecturers etc.), they have few opportunities to interact with faculty (commute time, over-protective parents/ guardians) and few opportunities to interact with other students due to commuting time, over-protective parents/guardians and low academic performance. They also lack adequate facilities including: classrooms, library, hostels, and badly ventilated rooms. For the most part, FCS faces poverty and financial problems leading to poor housing, prostitution, missing classes, tardiness and lack of fare.

The study was limited by time and small sample of students but even with those limitations, the study has yielded significant findings. According to the findings, FCS do face challenges especially in accessing affordable transportation and housing. This finding concurs with Horn & Berktold (1998) who argued that transportation issues are a large part of commuter student concerns. The study also found that FCS had little time to study and engage in extracurricular activities within the campus. This finding concurs with Tinto (1987) who indicated that commuter students spend limited time on campus and limited time creating relationships with other students, faculty, and staff; they have fewer opportunities to engage in quality interactions with these individuals. Participants also indicated the inability to interact with fellow students and faculty. This is consistent with Pascarella (1993) who found that not only was frequent contact with students outside the classroom difficult to obtain, but commuters often faced limited contact opportunities with faculty and staff members as well. The finding is also consistent with Astin(1983) who observed that as a result of not living in residence halls or spending a substantial amount of time on campus, commuter students miss out on these opportunities to "connect" to the university and other students and to enhance their learning and development.

The students in this study reported incidences of insecurities and sexual harassment from predators. It could be possible that the general community where this study was carried out is insecure and students are attacked more due to their higher academic status. The *matatu* touts they mentioned are often school dropouts but could have the same aspirations in terms of winning the affection of a college going woman. The aspect of having male lecturers as predators was also interesting. There are some anecdotal stories documented about "grades for sex" but more studies need to be done to unravel these phenomena.

There is no doubt that care has to be taken to ensure the academic success of commuter students in public institutions of higher learning. The students recommended that the university should invest on campus housing to make it more accessible and affordable for female students. Having students live in accommodation that is insecure, congested and inhabitable housing contradicts the university's strategic plan of making education accessible to all.

References

Astin, A.W. (1993). "What Matters in College?" *Liberal Education* 79:4–15.

George, D. Kuh, Robert, M. Gonyea, Megan, P. (2001). The Disengaged Commuter Student: Fact or Fiction? National Survey of Student Engagement. Indiana University Center for Postsecondary Research and Planning

Gleazer, E.J. (1980). The community college: Values, vision and vitality. Washington: American Association of Community and Junior Colleges.

Horn, L. J., and Berktold, J. (1998). *Profile of Undergraduates in U.S. Postsecondary Education Institutions: 1995-96.* Washington, DC: Office of Educational Research and Improvement, U.S. Department of Education (NCES 98-084).

Jacoby, B. (2000). "Involving Commuter Students in Learning: Moving from Rhetoric to Reality." In *Involving Commuter Students in Learning: New Directions for Higher Education No. 109,* ed. Barbara Jacoby. San Francisco: Jossey-Bass.

Noel, L., Levitz, R., & Saluri, D. (1985). Increasing student retention. San Francisco: Jossey Bass.

Pascarella, E. T., and Terenzini, P. T.(1991). *How College Affects Students.* San Francisco: Jossey-Bass.

Pascarella, E.T. (2001). Identifying excellence in undergraduate education: Are we even close? *Change, 33*(3), 19-23.

Tinto, V. (1987). *Leaving College.* Chicago: University of Chicago Press.

Villella, E.F., & Hu, M. (1991). A factor analysis of variables affecting the retention decision of non-traditional college students. *NASPA Journal,* 28(4), 334-341.

CHAPTER 4

CHALLENGES AND BARRIERS TO QUALITY EDUCATION FOR STUDENT MOTHERS IN KENYA'S PUBLIC UNIVERSITIES

Mary Mahugu

College Student Mothers

College student mothers face many obstacles and difficulties as they strive to balance the roles of being students and mothers (Brown & Amankaa, 2007). As can be expected, raising young children put a lot of demands on student mothers' time (perhaps) greater than the amount of time they spend in class. They must also study to achieve satisfactory academic performance. Pressures to perform in class are added to those they already feel from their home and child-rearing responsibilities (Brown & Amankaa, 2007). Being a student mother in college does not change social expectations for the student mother. She is expected to attend both anti-natal and post-natal clinics, give in assignments on time, do seminar presentations, and a host of other activities expected of a student. People may also view student mothers differently. Even if having children may have been a conscious choice, people may assume that the college mother was irresponsible in her social and sexual behavior (Buteau 2007).

As a student counselor, I have counseled student mothers handling crowded schedules. They must somehow balance the need to study and keep up the grades with the need to take care of their children and give them a happy, healthy environment in which to grow. Classes and the children's natal clinics may fall on the same post or prenatal days and time, leading to schedule conflict. Child care providers may leave without notice prompting the student mother to miss important engagements and even exams in order to take care of their infant. The college student mother has little time to care for their own physical and emotional health. Getting regular exercise, a healthy diet, and adequate sleep and rest may be impossible. Finding the time and a quiet place to study is often a challenge, and as such, often study does not begin until after the children are put to bed.

In addition, financial constraints are real challenges for most students that utilize our counseling services. The costs of tuition and fees, textbooks, laboratory fees, accommodation and transportation compete for the limited money set apart for rent, groceries, and child care. While student loans are available, they add to the financial burden unknown to college students who do not have children. Mounting debt is common among student mothers attending college. A mother without a supportive extended family or outside resources may be forced to make the heart-breaking decision to give up studies to cater for the child. In my role as a college counselor, I have witnessed many cases of missed seminar presentations, continuous assessment tests (CATS), examinations and field trips among student mothers. Although the university grants student mothers 21 days maternity leave, some students are not fully recovered to resume studies, leading to deferments. Those mothers with no additional financial support to cater for the extra expenses of hiring a house help and feeding her small family may drop out of their studies.

It can be deduced from these experiences that motherhood, while in college, affects career development by interfering with retention and progression of the student mother in her course of study.

Real difficulties exist in providing college student mothers with comparable education to that of their counter parts. As a student counselor in a large public university in Kenya, I have observed the personal, social and educational life being disrupted by the demands of pregnancy and/or parenting and most times require considerable individual determination, family support and supportive agencies for the student mother to resume or remain in college. Since this population is not the traditional students most educators and decision-makers envisioned when creating their institutions and policies, there are structural barriers for the progression and retention of student mothers in these institutions. There is no provision for "catch-up" education for those who may have missed out on education due to factors such as pregnancy and early marriage. Policies for granting aid and supporting students to succeed in their studies are gender blind. They do not take into consideration the unique needs of each gender. The blanket loans programs through state funding encourage institutions not to develop internal indicators that can help needy students to succeed especially the female student who is parenting while still in college. The questions to ask then are; what can be done to help college student mothers' progress with their education while maintaining a life of dignity? What can be done to eliminate/reduce the challenges/barriers for student mothers so as to facilitate/enhance their college experience?

Challenges to the Attainment of Quality Education

Access to a good quality education is acknowledged as a basic human right (Ojobo, 2008). Governments the world over are investing heavily in education to ensure that there are high enrollment and retention rates. Whereas enrollment rates continue to rise globally in the last three decades, over 403 million children under 17 years in the developing countries are out of school, more than 50% of whom are girls (FAWE NEWS, 2000). In Kenya, the situation is not any different. Currently the enrollment for girls in both primary and secondary schools stands at 49% and 47% respectively (UNESCO, 2008). Transition to tertiary institutions still remains low. It is estimated that the country has 198,119 University students of which approximately 80% are in public universities (Kenya National Bureau of Statistics, 2010). The overall proportion of female students remains low, at 36.6% of total enrolment in 2009. In public universities, the proportion of students who are female is 31% (Otieno & Colclough, 2009).

Higher Education in Africa- student retention and progression

Many students face challenges on the way to attaining a college education. However, student mothers face an especially daunting journey (Brown & Amankwaa, 2007). Real difficulties exist in providing student mothers with quality education (Pinilla & Samaria, 2005). The woman's personal, social and educational life may be disrupted by the demands of pregnancy and/or parenting and it can require considerable individual determination, family support and supportive agencies to resume or remain in college. Since they are not the traditional students most educators and decision-makers envisioned when creating their institutions and policies, these create barriers for the progression and retention of student mothers in these institutions (Pinilla & Samaria, 2005).

Haleman (2004) argues that education is the basis for the full promotion and improvement of the status of women. It empowers women by improving their living standard and it is the starting point for women's advancement in different fields of human endeavor (Ojobo, 2008). Yet the problem of poor academic performance and social exclusion of student mothers still exists in our colleges. Since low educational attainment will compound the barriers to employment resulting from difficulties of child care and of balancing responsibility for early motherhood and studies, there is need for more flexible arrangements for the pursuit of educational qualifications to ensure that motherhood while in college does not lead to further diminution of life chances.

Researchers have over the years conducted in-depth investigations to explain college student mothers do not perform as well as their counterparts (Riordan, 2002; Yakaboski, 2010; Chigona, & Chetty, 2008, Pinilla, & Samaria, 2005). The large body of knowledge generated indicates that student mothers in college face certain barriers that curtail their attainment of good quality college degrees within the stipulated time span. These barriers can be classified in to three broad areas (Yakaboski, 2010; Riordan, 2002)):

a) Stereotypes,

b) Barriers and

c) Support

Yakaboski (2010) conducted two focus group meetings with 21 student participants. The goal of using focus groups was to enable the participants to co-construct their meanings and experiences as self-identified college student mothers rather than having the research guided too much by the researcher and moderators. The single mother undergraduates "desired a stronger sense of support from faculty, staff, and peers: more family friendly events and campus services; more diversity in financial assistance; and more programming and day care options for children" (Yakaboski, 2010, p. 474).

Riordan (2002) used data from The Teen Parents Support Initiative (TPSI). Data was collected in consultation with TPSI project staff and participants parents. Other researchers have identified other factors such as the relationship that exists between young mothers' perceptions of the educational and employment opportunities available to them, teenage pregnancy and parenthood and lower levels of educational attainment (Riordan, 2002). According to Riordan (2002), lack of future employment or educational opportunities for young women means some may not see early motherhood as in any way damaging their future opportunities. Additionally, negative school experiences prior to or during pregnancy may also serve to sever already weak links between young parents and the formal educational system.

Stereotypes to single motherhood

Single mothers experience negative stereotypes as they negotiate postsecondary institutions. They face an undue amount of pressure because the dominant discourse about family creates stereotypes that "revolved around issues of family form, welfare participation and race" (Haleman, 2004, p. 772). Yakaboski, (2010) approaches the racial feminization of poverty from a positive perspective. Feminization of poverty posits that women, and specifically women of colour, are more likely to be the sole head of household for a family, thus having to bear all economic and societal pressures. Due to this access to and opportunity for higher education, advancement is more critical to this population not only for themselves as mothers and women but also for the next generation of children. Yet single mothers worry that their actions and presence are unwelcomed due in part to the marginalization of class issues. This dominant discourse creates an environment that victimizes many single mothers and sentences their children to a life at or below the poverty line. In the African setting, the issues of class and race may not feature prominently due to the fact that most governments do not have any welfare programs to assist the needy members of their communities, including student mothers.

Cultural, community and family values may impact upon young parents' decision whether to remain at home or return to education or employment. Communities may differ on the 'most acceptable' option for young mothers to follow – some may place greater value on young mothers 'staying at home' with their child while others may prioritize participation in employment or return to some form of part-time education (Buehler & O'Brien, 2011). Due to the social constructions of 'good mothering', young women may not wish to return to education during the early years of their child's life expressing a preference for remaining at home during these years. However, this preference may be driven by an understanding that this is what is expected of them (Phoenix, 1991).

Barriers to Attainment of Higher Education

Riordan (2002) argues that barriers limiting young parents' opportunities to participate in education and training can be classified as family, social and cultural obstacles including a lack of parental or familial support, social constructions of good mothering, cultural values, feelings of stigmatization and exclusion; and structural and institutional obstacles including exclusion from mainstream schooling, negative school experiences, childcare affordability and availability, financial needs and lack of external counseling and support programs. Identity conflicts also serve as a barrier to single mothers' college access and success (Riordan, 2002). Women are unique in their complex identity roles, and motherhood interacts with their college experiences. Women's competing identities suggest that student affairs practitioners approach programming for student parents slightly differently, including developing a plan that integrates the competing roles. Understanding this conflict is essential to creating policies and programs supportive of single-parent students (Yakaboski, 2002).

Socio-economic support

Single mothers often require a comprehensive suite of services, or wrap-around supports, since many face multiple risk factors. Given the right support from her college, a student parent is often able to flourish, choosing the progression of classes she needs, finding helpful advisers and counselors, getting involved with peer groups, and connecting with the campus programs that will benefit her the most as she balances her busy life (Women Employed, 2011). In general, retention rates and grades have also improved when low-income students have a coordinated network of services that includes academic counseling, progress monitoring, success workshops, and referrals to personal counseling. Services that help single-parent students and other non-traditional students surmount barriers to graduation could drastically improve the standard of living for these students and improve graduation rates. These academic and support services could include: financial aid; tutoring; academic advising; mentoring; career counseling; childcare; and referrals to food banks, counseling, and housing, (Women Employed, 2011).

The increasing numbers of women and adults entering college creates the need for higher education institutions to adjust programmatic support to improve retention. The retention of women and adults improves higher education diversity, thereby positively influencing all students.

Student mothers are an under-served social group whose social inclusion as a minority group is long overdue. Single student mothers often live at the intersection of a number of risk factors, which combine to create barriers that would be difficult for any college student to overcome. The purpose of this study was to explore ways of eliminating or minimizing these challenges so the student mothers can enjoy their college experience, perform well academically and complete their studies in a timely manner.

48

Methods

Setting: The study was carried out in a large public university with a majority of the students being government sponsored. The male to female ratio was 55% to 45%. Academic programs in this institution are fashioned after the traditional 8.00 AM to 5.00PM working hours. Only the essential services are extended beyond this time.

Sampling: A total of 14 students comprising of single student mothers, married student mothers, those with children and those who were pregnant participated in the study. They were identified through the University student mothers association that has a population of 40 registered mothers. The following is a short sample description of the students who participated in the detailed interviews. Names have been changed to ensure anonymity:

Kamene is a married student mother with three sons. She joined the University as a mature student when her last born son was two years. She commutes from home near the university. Her family lives on shared premises with her in-laws who are not at all happy with their daughter-in-law's decision to go back to school. She has this to say of her relationship with her in-laws;

> 'I get very little support from my in-laws.... They say I went back to study so I can look for other lovers there....' Kamene

Joy is a single student mother to a one and a half year old son. She was pregnant when she joined the university almost two years ago. Now in her third year of study, she has left the baby back at home with her mother. The father of the baby is a colleague in a different university. They are still together, though he is not able to support her financially.

Kate is a second year student who is five months pregnant. She has not shared this information with her family. She is afraid of their reaction. The father of her unborn baby has deserted her. As she struggles with morning sickness and poor appetite, she is afraid whether her poor state of health will affect the baby. She constantly misses classes due to her poor health. When questioned about what she was doing about her health, she said,

> '..... I went to the hospital and the doctor recommended that I get some nutritional supplements.....can't afford them, so I may just have to do without them...I hope the baby turns out to be okay....' Kate

Juanita is a single student mother in her second year of study. She gave birth to her son while in her first year of college. She still lives on rented premises outside campus with her son. Her family has constantly supported her and she is grateful to have them in her life.

Instruments

Focus Groups: The focus group discussions were organized around two thematic areas, namely: (a) challenges faced by the student mothers and how they affect their academic performance, and (b) how these challenges can be overcome. Two focus group discussions were held each lasting approximately one hour. Eight students participated in the discussions. The participants conducted and directed the discussions.

Individual interviews: The interview was a ten item schedule that sought to clarify issues that emerged during the focus group discussions. The items addressed the student mothers' experiences during and after the birth of their children. They also explored forms of support that the mothers received or lacked during this period. Ways in which student motherhood impacted on their academic performance were also explored. Finally the mothers were given a chance to suggest ways in which they would wish their needs as student mothers were met.

The proceedings for both the interview and the focus groups were recorded with consent and later transcribed for analysis.

Procedure

Two weeks prior to carrying out the research, I obtained permission from the Dean of students to collect data from a selected sample of fourteen student mothers. The data would be handled confidentially and consent sought from the selected students to participate in this research. I then distributed the consent letters to the student mothers participating in the research. The participants were assured that their responses would be kept confidential, their names would not be reported and they would remain anonymous. They were also free to withdraw at any time from the study without penalty. Once I got back the consent forms, I sent out a schedule of important dates. This included the dates and time for conducting the focus group discussions, and also the date and time for the interviews. The participants for the interviews were given an opportunity to select the most convenient time within the stipulated period. During the first week I conducted two focused group discussions on the theme – the challenges that student mothers face in college and how it impacts their academic performance, and how the challenges faced by the student mothers can be overcome. Each group discussion took approximately one hour. In the second week, I conducted detailed interviews with six mothers. I interviewed three students every day for two days. The interviews lasted approximately forty five minutes.

Results

In reviewing the data, a number of themes emerged:

a) social isolation;
b) lack of access to academic resources leading to poor performance;
c) inadequate funding and poverty;
d) challenges in balancing parenting and scholarly pursuits;
e) type and quality of accommodation for the student mothers;
f) medical welfare for the mother and child;
g) family support.

Social isolation

When the pregnancy became public knowledge, all participants reported that they were abandoned by their friends, both males and females. This feeling of abandonment was well summarized by two participants who shared:

> When my pregnancy began to show, my friends started to avoid me. I used to walk around campus alone. I lost appetite due to the morning sickness, and there was no one to share with about the difficulties I was going through. My friends went to the extent of discussing me, saying that cheap girls are the ones who got pregnant. I was so ashamed of myself and I started missing classes.... Joy

> After the birth of my child, I resumed back to college. A lot of ground had been covered in terms of class work. It was very difficult to get a friend to lend me notes to copy. Colleagues think you cannot perform well. They avoid you in group discussions because they imagine you have nothing to contribute... Juanita

Lack of access to academic resources leading to poor performance

The students interviewed commented that they had difficulties due to the long walk to classes. Getting some seating space in the lecture rooms was hard since classes are always full, and they could not walk fast enough or jostle to book some space for themselves.

51

This meant that they would sit outside the lecture halls most of the time, and this affected their academic performance. Two of the girls said that they lost a lot of weight due to morning sickness. This led to their missing many classes. On resuming classes, after the birth of their children, the girls noted that they had problems copying notes and trying to catch up. Lecturers did not offer remedial classes to those who were lagging behind in performance. Using the library in the evenings was also a challenge to the mothers since they needed to be at home at this time to take care of their babies. The mothers commented thus:

"The school organized an educational tour for one whole week. I could not travel since I had a breast feeding child. I wish they would have considered us during the planning.... The lecturers treat us just like other traditional students in total disregard of our uniqueness as full time students and mothers." Wanja

My maid disappeared two weeks to examinations...I was so confused and was forced to leave my child with anyone willing to help me. I didn't do well in the examination I sat for on that day ....' Joy

'I miss classes when the children are sick...get supplementary examinations at such times' Kate

'I got many Cs. I pray it will not get any worse' Kamene

Inadequate funding and poverty

All the student mothers agreed that finances were a major challenge. Most depended on funding from the Higher Education Loans Board, while others were assisted by parents. One mother who was on work study, said that she borrows money from friends and pays back when she gets paid after work study. Some mothers who were also married said that their husbands helped a little, and others also do gardening in the village. Another student mother who was also married noted that her husband's relatives were suspicious of her being away on campus. They saw campus as a way of having extramarital affairs. This prompted them to offer very little financial or social support to her. Financial demands tripled after the birth of the child. There were more mouths to feed, diapers to be purchased, medical expenses to pay when the baby is unwell and house helps to be paid. Without adequate support from their families, some mothers opted to defer their studies for a while.

There are times I have no food at all in my house. At such times, my babysitter runs away and am left with the double tragedy of missing classes and taking care of the baby. I applied for work-study and this has taken a toll on me since I have to divide my time to cater for three equally demanding chores; my baby, my work and my studies... Lucia

My babysitter treats me as her employer. She has no idea how difficult it is to put a meal on the table every day. Most times I have to skip lunch to save some money for our supper... Irene.

Challenges in balancing parenting and scholarly pursuits

On balancing time between parenting and studies all the mothers agreed that it was a very difficult task. Housework was a lot on top of the school assignments. The mothers could only study after the babies went to bed. This meant that they had to sleep late and wake up early, which was tiresome. Distance from hostel to class was far, so they would not manage to use the library in the evenings. All the mothers admitted to having enrolled the help of a house maid. This however came with its own challenges. The mothers put the challenges thus:

Walking from my small room outside campus to the lecture halls is quite far, I always get to class late. I have a house help who is a day scholar. She sometimes misses coming to work or comes in late and leaves early. So I have to do a lot of housework and I get very tired to read... Juanita.

I have a house help but since I am a student, the girls leave for greener pastures. I rarely use the library in the evenings since there is no one to watch the baby for me at this time... Wanja

She also wastes food and finances are limited... Joy

She runs away every other day... Kamene.

Type and quality of accommodation for the student mothers

The accommodation available outside campus is not friendly to the needs of the mother and child. The rooms are far from the lecture halls and other resources that the students use such as library, students centre and even the health unit. The mothers complained of noisy neighbors, who would keep on trying to take advantage of the mothers and keep on knocking on their doors. The environment is often dirty, and security was also poor. One mother noted that the rooms lacked the basic items like a bed and a reading table. In her own words, Juanita said:

> No, the environment is not friendly. Where I got a room there was no bed. We slept on the floor and the baby kept on falling sick due to the cold. The environment was dirty and the houses expensive... Juanita.

Medical welfare for the mother and child

Medical insurance in institutions of Higher learning are designed with the traditional student in mind. The student is expected to be single with no child. With the rising cases of student mothers who are married or single, this has posed a major challenge both to the institutions and the student mothers. Cases of student mothers being denied some anti-natal medical procedures have been reported. One mother put it thus:

> When I started attending ante-natal clinics, I was expected to pay for certain lab tests. When I enquired why I had to pay yet I was a student with a medical cover, I was informed that my medical cover is intended to cover only me but not for my unborn child. Most of the drugs used by expectant mothers such as mineral supplements are always out of stock. I have to buy over the counter.... Kate

Family support

On the amount and type of family support the mothers were getting, all the mothers agreed that their families were very supportive. They were offering both social and financial support. Other family members volunteered to baby sit while the mothers went to class. Six of the mothers had left their babies back at home with their family members as they came back to continue with their studies. One student put it thus;

> My family paid my hospital bill. My sister pays my house help's salary, my mother pays rent, and my brother provides food... Juanita

Discussion and Conclusion

The purpose of this study was to establish the challenges and barriers that affect the progression, retention and academic performance of student mothers in institutions of higher learning. The study also explored what needs to be done to help college student mothers' progress with their education while maintaining a life of dignity, and to eliminate/reduce the challenges/barriers for student mothers so as to facilitate/enhance their college experience.

Findings from this study indicate that student mothers face unique challenges and barriers as they juggle motherhood and their academic pursuits. The challenges include social isolation by their colleagues and significant others within and even outside the institutions of higher learning. They lack meaningful access to academic resources leading to poor performance. These include access to the library, participation in group work and field trips and also remedial teaching. Most student mothers do not have enough funds to meet their needs and those of their children. Even though a large number received some kind of support from their families, it was apparent that this was not enough to meet all their needs. Balancing parenting and scholarly pursuits was a major challenge for all the student mothers. This was compounded by the fact that securing professional house helps was difficult due to the financial constraints. The mothers were constantly fighting fatigue due to tight schedules. Accommodation for the student mothers was located far from the university facilities. It was expensive, dirty and insecure. Though the mothers had adequate medical insurance for themselves, their children lacked even the primary health care.

The study faced a number of limitations. I used purposeful and convenient sampling due to the small number of student mothers that were willing to participate in the research. The study also faced time constraint due to scheduling factors. However, these findings are consistent with other studies done on mothering while in college, which posit that student mothers face barriers limiting their opportunities to participate in education and training. These barriers include family, social and cultural obstacles including a lack of parental or familial support, social constructions of good mothering, cultural values, feelings of stigmatization and exclusion; and structural and institutional obstacles including exclusion from mainstream schooling, negative school experiences, childcare affordability and availability, financial needs and lack of external counseling and support programs.

These challenges and barriers could be due in part to policies and programs in our institutions that tend to be gender blind, and completely silent on student motherhood as a social category that faces unique challenges unlike the traditional single student. In Kenya, student mothers are presnet on our campuses, even though officially there are no statistics on how many they are. Acknowledgement of mothers in college then is a step towards social inclusion and needs to be strengthened. This can be done through introduction of academic and support services such as financial aid, tutoring, academic advising and mentoring; and also childcare; health care, counseling, and housing.

Further research on the role of the student fathers in supporting the student mothers in their academic pursuits should be done. There is also need to further explore college curriculums that are supportive of student mothers, with the aim of improving retention and progression of the student mothers in their academic pursuits. This will ensure that the student mothers complete their college degrees on time, and acquire quality degrees that guarantee them employment. As a result, the lives of the mothers and their offspring's will be improved, thereby improving the economy of the nation as a whole.

References

Brown, R. L. & Amankwaa, A. A. (2007). College females as mothers: Balancing the roles of student and motherhood. *The ABNF Journal* 18(1), p25-29

Buehler, C. & O'Brien, M. (2011). Mothers' Part-time Employment: Associations with Mother and Family Well-being. *Journal of Family Psychology.* 25(6): 895–906. doi: 10.1037/a0025993

Buteau, R. (2007). Balancing acts: A phenomenological study of single mothers who are successful students in higher education. In *Proceedings of the Adult Education Research Conference.*

Chigona, A.&Chetty, R. (2008). Teen mothers and schooling: lacunae and challenges. *South African Journal of Education* 28:261-281

FAWE News (2000).The news magazine about the education of girls and women in Africa 8 (3) 5

Haleman, D. (2004).Greater expectations: Single mothers in higher education. International Journal of Qualitative Studies in Education, 17, 769–784.

Kenya National Bureau of Statistics (2009).http://knbs.or.ke/downloads/pdf/Kenyafacts2009.pdf

Ojobo, J. A. (2008) Education: A catalyst for Women Empowerment in Nigeria. Retrieved from www.ajol.info/index.php/ejesc/article/viewFile/42995/26551

Otieno, W. and Colclough, C. (2009). Financing Education in Kenya: Expenditure, Outcomes and the Role of International Aid by," Research Consortium on Educational Outcomes & Poverty Working Paper, (25).

Phoenix, A. (1991) *Young Mothers?* Cambridge: Polity Press

Pinilla, B. & Samaria, M. (2005) Educational opportunities and academic performance: A case study of university student mothers in Venezuela, *Higher Education* 50: 299–322

DOI 10.1007/s10734-004-6356

Riordan, S. (2002) Young Parents in Education. The Centre for Social and Educational Research, Dublin Institute of Technology

UNESCO (2008).Institute for Statistics, Data Centre, 5. Retrieved from   http://www.nationmaster.com/country/ke-kenya/edu-education

Yakaboski, T. (2010).Going at it alone: Single-mother undergraduates' experiences. *Journal of Student Affairs Research and Practice, 47*(4), 463–481.

DOI:10.2202/1949-6605.6185

Women Employed, (2011).Single mothers and college success: creating paths out of poverty. Retrieved from http://www.womenemployed.org/working-lunch-2011

CHAPTER 5

EXAMINATION CHEATING IN PUBLIC INSTITUTIONS OF HIGHER LEARNING IN KENYA

Chedotum Kibet Ambrose (deceased)

Introduction

Research on examination anxiety has grown in recent years. Due to the increasing importance of test situations and their long-term significant consequences, examinations are creating educational, social, and clinical problems for many students (Chinta, 2005). As a lecturer at a public university I have lately observed increasing cases of examination anxiety and the twin consequence of examination cheating. The fact that there seem to be a large scale practice, compelled me to investigate the causes of the examination anxiety and what can be done to lessen its impact. Examination stress and test anxiety are pervasive problems in most educational institutions (Chinta, 2005). Alleviating test anxiety will also serve to counteract the diminished access to educational and occupational opportunities that is frequently experienced by test-anxious individuals. The purpose of this study was to investigate the impact of test anxiety among college students and what can be done to lessen the incidences of cheating.

Research context

There can be little doubt that examination anxiety occurs among college students. Oludipe (2009) defines anxiety as the chronic fear that occurs when a threatened event is in the offing but is unpredictable. This aspect of test anxiety can interfere with cognitive activity at the time of evaluation, such as memory recall, distractibility, and deficits in general concentration (McCabe, Trevino & Butterfield, 2001). Although most relaxation strategies address the emotionality component, it has been indicated that the worry components of test anxiety are the aspects that most adversely affect academic achievement (Gross, 1990).

Several studies have found significant differences with regard to general as well as specific test anxiety. Mwamwenda (1993) found no difference in test anxiety or academic achievement based on self-reported grade point average. There was nothing offered in the study with regard to actual grade point average. The study population was undergraduate students at a South African University. A year later, another study conducted by same researcher found a significant gender difference as well as lowered academic performance across genders for high test-anxious individuals (Mwamwenda, 1994).

Once again, the researcher used students from a South African University; however, these were graduate students, and academic achievement was based not on a self-report, but on actual scores on an educational psychology exam. Mwamwenda (1994) found that students perform more poorly on academic tests when experiencing test anxiety. This study also found that test preparation had no effect on the level of test anxiety and that highly test-anxious students performed poorly regardless of the amount of examination preparation.

Khalid and Hasan as cited in Rana & Mahmood (2010) conducted a study on a purposively selected sample of 187 undergraduate students to explore the relationship between test anxiety and academic achievement and "found that students with high academic achievement have low test anxiety scores and vice versa" (pg. 2). Chapell, Blanding, Takahashi, Silverstein, Newman, Gubi, and McCann, as cited in Rana & Mahmood (2010), conducted a study to explore the relationship between test anxiety and academic performance. They collected data from a large sample of graduate and undergraduate students and found a significant and negative relationship between test anxiety and academic achievement. Gierl and Rogers (1996) conducted a study using Canadian high-school students. The base study used 724 (335 male and 389 female) "school-leaving" Canadian high-school students. The overall results found no significant difference between males and females in general test anxiety for all ages studied. Davis and Ludvigson (1995) in turn present a twofold way of reducing cheating in the long run, namely by a) using positive reinforcement and b) by encouraging and fostering the students to acquire an outlook on life that will prevent them from cheating. Even though a lot of research has been done on examination anxiety globally, little is known about the subject in Kenya. The purpose of this study was to investigate how examination anxiety impacts college students in Kenya and whether it is causes examination cheating.

Methodology

Thirteen unstructured questions were given to 50 students comprising 10 first years, 9 second years, 10 third years, 10 fourth years and 11 postgraduate students at the School of Human Resource. The first question asked about gender, the second one was on age, the third one was whether they have ever been faced with any anxiety, then fourth one was whether the anxiety was examination related, the fifth one was the type of examination anxiety the participants suffered and the amount of test anxiety experienced, the other question was the participant's test anxiety affect the level of academic performance, the seventh question was, how does respondent's test anxiety affect the level of academic performance and why do Females have higher levels of worry as well as higher levels of emotionality, whether there is difference of test anxiety between males and females, whether the learning styles cause test anxiety, whether age is a factor that affects examination anxiety.

Findings

In reviewing the data collected for this study, a few themes emerged including:

a)   methods used for cheating;

b)   non cheaters, and

c)   gender and age differences when it came to cheating.

Methods used to cheat

There was a general agreement that students frequently cheat in examination using different methods. The most frequently method used was copying material for course-work from a book to "*Mwakenya*". This is the process whereby the students make short notes that can be well hidden from the instructor or the examination proctor but accessible to them during the exam. Other students shared that they paraphrased material from another source without acknowledging the original author. They also shared that they copied each other's work. Other students made frequent visits to the bathroom and others used their cell phones to do internet search (usually using Google) for answers or to communicate with colleagues.

Non cheaters

While cheating was rampant, some participants in this research indicated a reluctance to cheat because they thought cheating was immoral and dishonest. Others did not distance themselves from cheating, only that it was not considered or regarded as useful. Comments such as "I never thought of it" and "Situation did not arise" were shared. Others feared detection and getting caught as well summarized by one participant who said "shame/embarrassment at being caught" and another one "fear of detection/punishment"

Gender Differences

Out of the participants that were involved from first years to postgraduate twenty four were females and twenty six were male. The students' responses to the items depicting various cheating behaviors were in most cases similar for both genders; that is, there are almost no differences between female and male student's responses in this respect. Two items, however, had different reactions that are related to differences by gender. One of these items was "taking unauthorized material into an examination *(Mwakenya)."* The result indicates that there are clear differences between female and male students' ways of responding to cheating in the form of taking unauthorized material in the testing situation. Among the female students only 12 admitted to the behavior while 21 of the male students said 'Yes' to having carried out the cheating. The outcome points to small differences between the female and male ways of selecting the reason for their behavior regarding "Taking unauthorized material into an examination". The twenty one male students selected "Fear of failure as a reason" for this cheating behavior while no girls shared that reason. Also "It would be unfair to other students," were chosen by five male students but none of the female students. Among the female students reasons like "To increase the mark," "Laziness", "I would not know how to go about it" and "Situation did not arise/not applicable to my course" were chosen by a few female students but no male student. A relatively large difference between female and male ways of choosing among the reasons for explaining the Yes/ No-answer can be found for reason "I never thought about it", where five female students selected that reason while it attracted twenty one of the male students. Also "It would devalue my achievement" was chosen by a larger proportion female student (fifteen) than male students (five).

Age differences

There was no marked difference in frequency of cheating as far as age was concerned. One mature student in the privately sponsored program shared "that since they are very busy with home chores, work assignments and academic work weighed on them, this gave them the pressure to cheat as they were also under pressure to pass examinations since they were paying through their noses". On whether the students have ever faced any anxiety, some of them did indicate that yes they have experienced when examinations are approaching and they have not paid fees, the pressure of passing examinations was a major source of anxiety. The type of examination anxiety they experience included fidgeting, sweating in the palms, increased heartbeat, blanking out, headache and restlessness which affects negatively their level of academic performance as they do not perform well hence they are tempted to cheat in exams. When a student has well prepared examination timetable they're able to reduce examination anxiety hence are less likely to cheat.

Discussion and Conclusion

From these findings it is clear that examination cheating is a major problem among college students. It is a cancer that needs to be arrested before quality of education is compromised. The overall frequency of cheating reported in this study does not differ significantly from the ones reported by previous researchers (Chinta, 2005) and can, hence, be taken as a further proof of the fact that the overall cheating rates seem to be fairly consistent among college students. Time pressure was cited as the most frequent reason for cheating. A few mentioned the wish to increase the mark as the most frequent reason for cheating. The full time students' attribute their cheating to laziness and extenuating circumstances considerably more often than their mature peers, who, in turn, seem to fear failure more and also tend to justify their behavior with the reason "everybody does it". Out of these differences it is easy to create a caricature image of the cheating full time student as an ambitious person, who wishes to perform well and of the mature student who mainly cheats because it seems to be the easiest way to go about the studies.

Mature students seem to have two main reasons for not cheating one being that it would have been pointless/unnecessary and that it would have been immoral/dishonest. The immorality aspect is mentioned as the most frequently used deterrent among the mature students, but the second most frequently used is that the student never thought of it, closely followed by the reason that the situation didn't arise or wasn't applicable. Again, then, the mature students seem to be more focused on the outcome/the result of the cheating behavior as compared to the regular full time student.

Even though morality is one of the most frequently used reasons for not cheating in both of the groups, the "potential cheater-reasons", i.e. the ones giving I never thought of it, the situation didn't arise and/or it was unnecessary/pointless, were more. In connection to the fact that the reasons shame/embarrassment at being caught and fear of detection/punishment were used quite infrequently, this implies that it is of the utmost importance to reduce the opportunities of successful cheating, e.g. by creating individual examinations and other assessment tasks that demand creativity and originality, not just reproduction. The fact that embarrassment is such an infrequent reason also implies that neither mature nor full time students feel responsible for the "code of honor" of their academic institutions. Hence, by establishing a functioning code of honor one could most likely reduce the instances of cheating remarkably, since the socio-moral climate is known to affect the behavior of students more effectively than their own level of moral development (McCabe, Trevino & Butterfield, 2001). The reduction of opportunities for successful cheating is, of course, the most immediate way of reducing cheating, but in the long run that measure will not suffice. According to the findings in this study, there is a gap between the notions of morality and correctness as held by society and university staff and the notions of these phenomena held by the students (McCabe, Trevino & Butterfield, 2001). It is therefore necessary to spell out which the common rules are and also ensure they are followed. To go further, it is imperative to stress the importance of moral education for moral development in order to secure a functioning society, presuming that that is what is desired. Except the minor gender differences on some items, there were, however, also weak, but significant positive correlations between the overall tendency to cheat and year of study, the perception of how much other students cheat and reason for studying. These results implies that academic misconduct, at least to some extent, may be epidemic and that students' reasons for not cheating are gradually worn down when they see fellow students cheat, without being caught. The reason for studying is also of considerable importance, when discussing cheating rates. An obvious way of reducing cheating in our faculties would be to ensure that only intrinsically motivated students are admitted to institutions of higher learning. The question is then: How do we control for that, and do we really want to; It is all linked to the kind of professionals we want to educate.

Conclusion

Academic staff can no longer presuppose that students know and behave according to unwritten moral rules or an inner code of honor. One obvious way of reducing cheating in Kenyan universities is to spell out what rules and codes the students are subjected to. Such a document ought, however, to be carefully thought out and produced in co-operation with the students, in order to establish it as a "code of honor, otherwise it will only fill the purpose of a list of potentially successful cheating behaviors. According to previous research, students' moral behavior and ethical reasoning seems to develop under continuous education (Davis and Ludvigson, 1995). I am convinced that this influence can be made stronger through focused attention to the area and an open ethical dialogue, not in any specific course, but as every teacher's concern. This would create a good socio-moral environment for moral development, which is what universities ought to foster in their students, since that is something they will need in their everyday life as well as in their professional activities, and of which society will benefit or suffer in the long run. Even though the personal factors causing or preventing cheating are probably the primary ones, it is also a good idea to try to reduce or eliminate the external factors that seem to cause cheating. One of the major external reasons for cheating was time pressure. That ought to be quite easily remedied through courses/supervision in studying technique and discipline, as well as a better co-ordination of courses and examinations between university staff. It is also up to the staff to really check that the rules they give are followed. Such a behavior signals that the rules are judged as important and might awaken conscience in the students, or at least make the "cheating alternative" less attractive and not easy to carry out. In this case it is, in fact, most important to catch the small fish.

References

Chinta, R. (2005). Exam anxiety effect on exam performance: An empirical replication in the Middle East. Eryan Hellas Ltd.

Davis, S. F., & Ludvigson, H. W. (1995). Additional Data on Academic Dishonesty and a Proposal for Remediation. Teaching of Psychology, 22, 119-121.

Gierl, M., & Rogers, W. (1996). A confirmatory factor analysis of the Test Anxiety Inventory using Canadian high school students. *Educational and Psychological Measurement, 56,* 315-324.

Gross, Thomas F. (1990). General test and state anxiety examinations: State is not test anxiety. *Educational Research Quarterly, 14,* 11-20.

Khalid, R., & Hasan, S. S. (2009). Test anxiety in high and low achievers. *Pakistan Journal of Psychological Research, 24*(3-4).

McCabe, D. L., Treviño, L. K. & Butterfield, K. D. (2001). Cheating in Academic Institutions: A Decade of Research. *Ethics & behavior,* 11(3), 219–232

Mwamwenda, T. (1993). Gender differences in test anxiety among South African University students. *Perceptual and Motor Skills, 76,* 554-560.

Mwamwenda, T. (1994). Gender differences in scores on test anxiety and academic achievement among South African University graduate students. *South African Journal of Psychology, 24,* 228-231.

Oludipe, B. (2009). Influence of test anxiety on performance levels on numerical tasks of secondary school physics students: *Academic Leadership: Online Journal, 7* (4)

Rana R. A. & Mahmood N. (2010). The relationship between test anxiety and academic achievement. *Bulletin of Education and Research.* December 2010, Vol. 32, No. 2 pp. 63- 74

SECTION TWO

CHALLENGES EXPERIENCED BY FACULTY

CHAPTER 6

GENDER DISPARITIES AMONG FACULTY AT SCIENCE-BASED PROGRAMS IN KENYA'S PUBLIC UNIVERSITIES

Fatuma Daudi

Introduction and Background

This study was motivated by my personal experiences as a girl growing up, as a secondary school science educator and as a lecturer in a science-based department in a public university in Kenya. Each stage of my education has clearly been marked by gender disparity. At one point I was the only female teacher serving as the head teacher in a girl's school while the rest of teachers, sixteen to be precise, including the deputy head teacher were male. The story was the same in my studies. For instance, for my masters' degree, I was the only female in a class of four students. In my present position at an institutions of higher learning, the story is the same. In the school of environmental studies where I work, there were only six women in comparison to 21 male faculty members at the time of this study.

A study carried out by the Forum for African Women Educationists (FAWE) in Western, Eastern and Southern African found out that women were underrepresented at all levels in African Universities (Salo, 2003). In the early years of schooling the number of girls to boys are almost equal, at least at the primary level. The situation however, is slightly different in secondary and tertiary levels, where ratio of girls to boys reduce dramatically. The disparity is clearly marked at all the stages of women's education as well as in career especially in the male-dominated fields like science and technology (Varpaloti, 2010). This trend is also common in the institutions of higher learning especially at university level. Nguyen (2000) contends that higher education supplies the best resources for the labor force; it influences current leaders and prepares future leaders. Manuh (1995) argues that more research is needed to explore gender relations more deeply in order to explain the ideological and material basis for women's continuing subordination.

The main aim of this study was therefore, to investigate the experiences of women lecturers in a science-based university program as a basis for understanding the causes of gender disparities and to provide practical solutions to close the gender gap.

Gender Inequalities in the Workplace

Acker (1990) argues that a gendered organization means that advantage and disadvantage, exploitation and control, action and emotion, meaning and identity, are patterned through and in terms of a distinction between male and female, masculine and feminine. Gender is not an addition to ongoing processes, conceived as gender neutral. Rather it is an integral part of those processes that cannot properly be understood without an analysis of gender. Therefore, the gendering of organizations can be attributed to the wider social norms concerning the proper relations between men and women. Similarly, Morley (2005) argues that gender inequality is a feature of social relations in most societies. It is linked to poverty, violence, the labor market, health, housing, and education. It structures the relations of production and reproduction and is inextricably linked with knowledge construction and dissemination.

Gender differentiation and roles are nurtured and molded by the society, thus are socially constructed. It is through culture and the accompanying customs that the mindsets of men are set towards what it means to be a man. Wafula, (2012), talking of his personal experiences on how he was raised differently by his mother in the absence of his father, says that these beliefs about what it means to be a man or woman are formed so early in life. At early age of eight or less, boys have been already 'formatted' to subscribe to the tenets of a world characterized by negative masculinity and the dominance of women and girls. These cultures, reinforced by religion, have contributed to the marginalization women and girls all over the world.

A study carried out at three universities in Ghana found women in faculty and administration positions to be highly underrepresented (Adusah, 2008). Kamau (1999), explaining disparities in reference to women academics in Kenya, argues that women experience a multiplicity of role conflict and negative traditional culture which defines them as social deviants causing their exclusion from informal academic networks, suffering excessive workloads and marginalized by strong patriarchal culture. This study further revealed that women accomplishments were undervalued and discounted, which results in low esteem thus lack of confidence on the part of the women (Kamau, 1999).

The issue of women's access to higher education came up on the global political agenda in 1998 when UNESCO convened a World Conference on Higher Education at which a panel of experts reviewed the progress made in gender equality in higher education since the Beijing Conference. The document *Higher Education and Women: Issues and Perspectives* prepared for the UNESCO conference identified two central areas related to women in higher education which needed the attention of researchers and policy makers. These, according to UNESCO, are fewer enrollment by women in higher education and the absence of gender dimension in the higher education curriculum (UNESCO, 1999). The participants at the World Conference on Higher Education (UNESCO, 1999) underscored the role of higher education in the enhancement of women's participation in the sector. Article 4 of the World Declaration on Higher Education for the 21ˢᵗ Century (UNESCO, 1999) called for the elimination of all gender stereotyping in higher education at all levels and in all disciplines in which women are under-represented. Women's active involvement in decision-making in higher education was emphasized. The participants at the conference recommended that by 2010 university chairs, professors, and heads of department posts should be filled by men and women on an equal basis (UNESCO, 1999). This vision has not been realized in most of the universities in the world (in general) and Kenya (in particular).

Rathgeber (2003) contends that the number and proportion of women as consumers of higher education is increasing, but the number of women as providers of higher education remains low at the senior level and in a number of key disciplines. The status of women in universities in sub-Saharan Africa is a reflection of women's position in society. Women are underrepresented in universities in sub-Saharan Africa, and those who are able to pursue higher education concentrate on traditional female fields, such as education, arts, humanities and social sciences. In almost all sub-Saharan African countries, female teaching staff are few in number and comprise less than 10% of the faculty at the senior professorial level (Rathgeber, 2003).

Women in Higher Education

Higher education is expanding internationally both in response to state investment in the knowledge economy and as a consequence of new private and offshore providers.

The Task Force on Higher Education and Society (2000) emphasizes that knowledge is a springboard for economic growth and development, making the promotion of a culture that supports its creation and dissemination an essential task. If any society is to succeed in this globalized economy, then a collective contribution from and participation of all citizens is a prerequisite. Many international communities have recognized the importance of gender issues. Gender issues are not only a matter of social justice but good economics. In general, although the gender gap is narrowing globally, more women than men remain illiterate. In developing countries, in particular, women tend to be less educated, work longer hours, and are paid less. Women make up one-half of the world's population, perform two-thirds of the world's work hours, yet everywhere they have fewer resources and are poorly represented in decision-making positions (Kolárová, 2006). Research indicates that in most developing countries, women are left behind in educational training, scientific knowledge, and technological literacy and are therefore at a disadvantage. Women need a strong foundation in education to compete favourably for positions in higher education which is a major reason why they are not employed in institutions of higher education.

Methods

Participants

Participants were selected through purposeful sampling, which is dominant strategy in qualitative research. Patton (2002) asserts that the logic and power of purposeful sampling lies in selecting information-rich cases for in-depth study. In this study, the main focus was to understand the experiences of women in higher education thus, the involvement of women who teach in the School of Environmental studies at the College. "Information rich-cases are those from which one can learn a great deal about issues of central importance to the purpose of inquiry" (Patton, 2002).

Others who were interviewed are women who have worked at the school for more than fifteen years with experiences of having worked with different administrators and women faculty members. This included secretaries, office messengers and administrators. This group was resourceful as they had a lot of information owing to their interaction with the faculty members and administrators.

Data Collection Techniques

Qualitative inquiry, which focuses on meaning in context, requires a data collection instrument that is sensitive to underlying meaning when gathering and interpreting data. Patton (2002) reveals that qualitative findings grow out of three kinds of data collection: in-depth, open-ended interviews, direct observation, and written documents. Glesne (2005) agrees with the fact that the use of multiple data collection methods contributes to the trustworthiness of data. The data for this study was obtained through interviews, open-ended questionnaires, observation and document analysis.

Document analysis was used to gather information from other studies as well as documents such as staff files[1]. Also reviewed were newsletters, reports, timetables (both teaching and examination) and the university gender policy. The need for this research and the real intentions as being solely for the sake of the betterment of all the faculty members was explained. All participants signed an informed consent form and were assured confidentiality and anonymity. They were told the study was voluntary and they could withdraw without penalty.

Data Analysis and Results

The main themes that emerged through analysis of the data included: low number of women in academic positions; women's early life experiences; causes of the disparities and attributes that assisted and enabled women faculty members to succeed.

Low Number of Women in Academic Positions

There are disparities between male and female employees at the university as shown in the documents analyzed, which included files, newsletters, and teaching and examination timetables.

The results show that women represented 21% and 20% of faculty and administrators, respectively, of university employees. At the School of Environmental Studies the number of women in teaching positions were 5 against 21 male in permanent employment. Those who are either on contract or on part time teaching were 3 females against 10 males. This translated into 80.7% to19.2% and 76.9% to 23%, respectively.

---

1   Official statistics on hiring by gender were obtained.

Women Early Experiences and the Causes of Disparities

The majority of respondents cited conflicts in managing their multiple roles as mothers, wives and workers. They also cited issues of interrupted careers, lack of mentoring and networks as key causes of gender disparities at the university level.

Rose (not her real name) said the following about her background, "I grew up in a polygamous family. My sister and I were the only children of my mother who was the only daughter in her family". This she said made her witness gender issues right from when she was a child. She noted that girls were not considered as important as boys, thus much preference given to the boys.

In agreement with her colleague, Immaculate (not her real name) shared that she was the only daughter among her three siblings. Her parents gave preferential treatment to the boys for the simple belief that they carried the family name "as opposed to me who was to be married to become part of another family". This made her parents take her brothers to very prestigious boarding schools while she went to the local public school as a day scholar. She said that her parents were "claiming that they were protecting me and were also looking for funds to take me to the same school one day, which never materialized and it was from then I realized that boys had more chance than I did and this made me feel intimidated". However, this motivated her to work and perform well just like her brothers. Being the only girl among the boys made her assertive and she had fight for her 'space' in order to survive. This is a virtue that she retains to date, and which has enabled her withstand male attitudes even from male student who can be a nuisance just because a woman is teaching them. What comes out clearly from this is that parents have a great role to play in moulding and shaping the future of their children. Another participant noted that "after my undergraduate course I did not think of further education, I only aspired to be a teacher or a nurse and build a family until my father encouraged me to proceed to do a masters degree which acted as the basis for my quest to proceed to attain a doctoral degree".

While the above sentiments indicate the socialization aspect by the society, it also clearly emphasizes the role of parents in what one becomes and attains in future thus the need for parents to take their responsibilities and role towards a better and equitable society.

Lack of mentors and role models

Another major cause of the disparity noted was lack of mentors or role models. All the women lecturers interviewed failed to identify any role model or mentor in their lives. The only figures mentioned in the study as inspirational were either the fathers or the mothers who in one way, or the other, inspired the women lecturers to excel and be what they have become. There were no female role models and mentors in the lives of the women lecturers interviewed. Either, they were not there or were hostile given the experiences they had gone through themselves. In fact those they found teaching were hostile to the fellow women, as explained by Immaculate who said "...no role model, there was one who was anti-women as she could not see, let alone interact with the female students or co-workers". She attributed this to jealousy and not wanting other women to join in teaching so that she could remain dominant; thus she saw others as competitors. Immaculate reported that she worked hard to excel just like her brothers who she described as "academic giants", saying that she was motivated to join the university only when her brother joined the University of Nairobi, one of the prestigious universities in Kenya. The stories he told her about his experiences at the university gave her the urge to join as well. At the time, she only aspired to complete a first degree.

Bennedictor (not her real name) was motivated by the fact that she wanted to try and find out if she could manage higher education. It was just a trial but she managed, though the journey was long and tough as she found out. This clearly shows the virtue of determination that helps the few women faculty members to get through the system which is otherwise difficult.

Lack of Networks and Exposure

Attitude was another constraint that was noted as inhibiting women from aspiring to venture into teaching at institutions of higher learning. Observations made on relationships within the work place indicated that, attitude from the male lectures, other staff and students towards the female lecturers was not pleasant. Women were treated as incompetent even in cases where they were out rightly brighter, more hardworking and more committed than their male colleagues. The culture of viewing women as playing second fiddle to men appears to be common and thus explains this attitude. Such attitudes tended to demoralize women, even those who otherwise had needed ambitions to succeed. This could be attributed to the 'male stereotype syndrome', as one female lecturer commented "male stereotype is dominant despite dealing with educated men…" The male faculty members do not engage women in projects and activities to give learning experiences and confidence to them. Thus women faculty members lack exposure and experiences needed to help them grow in the career.

Hostile Work Environment

Another challenge is the employment system which was described as unpleasant and not women friendly. In the first place the vetting committees for jobs hiring were dominated by men. This was compounded by lack of standardized procedures for the committees, leaving the process vulnerable to manipulation. Female lecturers lacked networks. While the male lecturers enjoy strong networks among themselves they did not incorporate their female colleagues. It is common to find that men have several projects but they hardly involve female lecturers, considering them either as a liability or nuisance in terms of being thorough and strict in their operations; incompetency or laziness.

Attributes that Assisted and Enabled Women Faculty Member to Succeed

Despite all handicaps some women have made it and are in academic positions at the university. Regarding the reasons behind their success many female lecturers cited and mentioned their parents. In most cases one parent was instrumental in their success, either the father or the mother; others emulated their mothers who were hardworking despite disadvantaged situations. This drove them to work hard and achieve their goals. These women were found to be hardworking, patient and committed to their work.

Rose, who served as head of department one time, asserts that "the experience of female lecturers is not easy nor sweet". She narrated her story on how she was appointed a head of department. The authorities had preferred someone else from another department. This is despite that she was qualified and had several years' experience commensurate with requirements of the job. The plan did not work as the university rule could not allow this to happen thus she got the opportunity. This advocates for organizations to uphold rules and policies, which in most cases are there but not adhered to. For example, gender policy at national and institutional levels exist but at times not upheld.

Once on the job, her work was not smooth sailing as she did not get support from the male lecturers. It was a struggle that saw her look for office space, furniture and other equipment on her own with a lot of struggle. This came about due to her administrative skills and her assertiveness in making herself clear and focused on the task.

The study findings pointed out characteristics that aided female lecturers as hard work, honesty, accuracy, being knowledgeable, being a team player and good time keepers.

All in all it was noted that such successful women were very honest and dedicated to their work compared to male colleagues. They articulated issues with boldness and with courage without fear or favour. This was evident from the fact that few as they were, all the female lecturers were given extra responsibilities in addition to their teaching loads. In fact, each of the members interviewed was in two or three committees in chairing capacity, which was not the case for the male lecturers who were busy with other group or individual projects that were beneficial to them directly. This clearly illustrates the potential of the female lecturers despite not being given the chance.

Discussion and Conclusions

The findings of this study point at culture as the overall and dominant factor in explaining why there are few female lecturers in the universities. It is important also to appreciate that culture is constructed and is dynamic, thus can be reconstructed to reflect best practices from experience. There is a need, therefore, for people to change their attitude if at all meaningful change can be expected to occur to realize gender parity at the university level and all other spheres of life. Myths and stereotypes, often used by various cultures, need to be challenged. This would encourage women to take up roles and also share their experiences which should be used as a guide to improving the situation.

The role of mentoring cannot be emphasized enough. The results of this study showed that the women lecturers did not have role models and mentors in their fields of endeavour. Mentorship culture and programs should be started at various schools to instill these practices to all members within and outside these institutions.

The university policy advocates for equal opportunity for all and, in order to deal with historical imbalances and injustices, calls for affirmative action. This has been interpreted to mean that women who are not qualified are allowed into jobs for the sake of numbers.

But this is not necessarily the case. The poor perception of affirmative action leads to situations where even capable women are viewed with suspicion and looked down upon.

The results also indicated that women are dedicated and good at what they do. In the words of one male administrator 'more women should join the teaching and other jobs at the university because they are accurate, honest, hardworking, team players and good time managers'.

The findings showed that women are capable and have the potential if given a chance. Policy makers and opinion leaders need to change their perception and give women the chances they so rightfully deserve. Women lecturers should also do away with preconceived fears that they have been programmed with and have come to believe. Sadie (2005) advanced the argument that at the bottom of the constraints that women face, is the patriarchal system where decision-making powers are in the hands of males. In the African context, traditional beliefs and cultural attitudes regarding the role and status of women in society are still prevalent, and many women are part of this system. As such, they find it difficult to dislocate from this culture and tradition lest they become ostracized. Despite women's education and entry into the job market, the woman's role is typically one of a homemaker.

The saying that 'women are their own enemies' can possibly be explained by the issue of lack of mentorship and role models. Equally, those who have excelled are hostile and do not encourage other women. In fact they were said to be bad i.e. sadists who made the lives of the other women lecturers a nightmare in terms of harassing them, and in the process demoralizing them. These women should realize that there are many opportunities and that others will only help, and make work easier and productive for all. They should not view colleagues as threats but opportunities to improve the work situation owing to the experiences and quality they bring to the work environment.

References

Acker, J. (1990). Hierarchies, jobs, bodies: A theory of gendered organizations. Gender and Society. V4 (2) 139 - 158.

Augustina, A. K., (2008). Experiences of Women in Higher Education: A Study of Women Faculty and Administrators in Selected Public Universities in Ghana, unpublished dissertation, Ohio University

Amal, A M, (2012), Interview with Al jazera, (July, 2012)

Debri H., (und) Diversifying the Faculty: Faculty Recruitment in Higher Education; Research findings on Diversity and Affirmative Action; AAC & U for the Ford Foundation

Kamau, N. (1999). Outsiders Within: Experience of Kenyan Women in Higher Education. Published by African Resource Centre

Manuh, T. (1995). Higher education, condition of scholars and the future of development in Africa, *CODESRIA Bulletin*, 3 & 4

Massachusetts Institute of Technology (MIT) (2001). A report on the status of women faculty in the School of Science and Engineering. Retrieved from http://web.mit.edu/faculty/reports/pc/

Patton, M. Q. (1985). Quality in qualitative research: Methodological principles and recent development. Paper Presented at the American Educational Research Association Conference, Chicago, IL.

Patton, M. Q. (2002). Qualitative research and evaluation methods. Thousand Oaks, CA: Sage Publications.

Piirto J. (2000). Why Are They So Few? Creative Women; Visual Artist, Mathematicians, Scientist, Musicians.

Rathgeber, E. M. (2003). Women universities and university-educated women: The current situation in Africa. In D. Teferra & P. G. Altbach (Eds.), African higher   education: An international reference handbook (pp. 82-92). Bloomington, IN: Indiana University Press.

Sadie,Y.(2005). Women in political decision-making in the sadc region.*Agenda, 65*, 17-31 publisher

Taskforce on Higher Education and Society (2000). Higher education in developing countries: Peril and promise. Washington, DC: World Bank.Author

UNESCO/Commonwealth Secretariat (1999). Women in higher education management. Paris, France: UNESCO.

Varpalotai, A (2010). The Status of Women in Canadian universities and the role of faculty unions. Forum on Public Policy: Universrity of Western Ontarion, Canada

Wanjala W.(und), 'Am indeed a Man". Retrieved from www. coexistkenya.com on 17th April, 2012.

CHAPTER 7

GENDER DISPARITIES IN DECISION MAKING LEVELS AT PUBLIC UNIVERSITIES IN KENYA: THE CASE OF MOI UNIVERSITY

Walter Kodipo

Introduction and Background

Gender disparity refers to statistical differences in the possessions, statuses, and opportunities between men and women. For instance, the raw statistic on the average income of men and women somewhat famously has women making around three quarters of the income of men. This is before factoring in such things as culturally influenced voluntary unemployment, differences in types of careers, and other important "in between" factors. There are arguments regarding the significance of these factors and the extent of their impact on gender disparities. Interpreted for Moi University, higher level education for female members of staff should be a set goal if at all gender parity at the higher echelon of the management is to be realized. It is important to remember that women are often denied the benefit of education in favour of their male siblings at an early stage of their lives. This is a reality which is common place in most African communities.

When women get absorbed in the labor market such as in the universities they tend to stagnate in the positions at which they were hired. They are unable to compete effectively with their male colleagues for promotions because of low levels of education which leads to a situation where there are more male than female staff at decision making levels in the governance structures of the university. Perhaps their academic level at entry point or failure by the university governance to recognize their potential has led to low academic progress.

Whereas under the new constitution of the republic of Kenya (promulgated in 2010), female standing in the society is legally protected, it will take time before their rights in various spheres of life including that of education are fully addressed:

All State organs and all public officers have the duty to address the needs of vulnerable groups within society, including women, older members of society, persons with disabilities, children, and youth, members of minority or marginalized communities, and members of particular ethnic, religious or cultural communities. The State shall enact and implement legislation to fulfill its international obligations in respect of human rights and fundamental freedoms. *(The Constitution of Kenya, Article 43 (3 & 4), 2010)*

Higher level of education is important in terms of middle level staff being promoted to senior cadres. Education is the principal means through which poor and marginalized individuals can break the vicious cycle of poverty and participate effectively in society, (Njogu & Orchardson-Mazrui 2006). Promotion of gender equality in education is essential for human resource development. The question to ask then is whether a female middle level staff at Moi University is able to access the professional development necessary to ensure promotions to higher levels of decision making structures.

Theoretical Framework and Review of Literature

The study is anchored on structural-functional theory which states that: different institutions and structures in a society form a function like part of a social machine (Merton, 1968). A common analogy by Herbert Spencer presents parts of society as organs that work toward the proper functioning of the body as a whole.

The structural-functional theory was essential in the understanding of the position of female staff in the university hierarchy. Moi University female middle level staff form an important cog in the wheel of the university's administrative and academic operations. The right to education is not a privilege but a fundamental right (UNESCO, 2000). This is also enshrined in the Kenyan Constitution *(The Constitution of Kenya, Article 43 (3 & 4).* In allocating resources, the State shall give priority to ensuring the widest possible enjoyment of the right or fundamental freedom having regard to prevailing circumstances, including the vulnerability of particular groups or individuals. The survival of our society depends, to a large extent, on the education of our people irrespective of their age or ethnic orientation. Education is a tool for empowering the people everywhere including those working in the institutions of higher learning.

The state is the central actor in any claim to the right to education:

It is the prime duty-bearer and the prime implementer; it is the guarantor; and it is the state's signature vis-à-vis the international norms and standards which binds it to respect protect and fulfill the right to education. The state must therefore be judged or challenged on its central text on the right to education, whether this be the constitution, the laws or policies (http://www.right-to-education.org/country).

The Employment Act, No. 11 of 2007 expressly prohibits discrimination and harassment of actual and prospective employees on the basis of sex in section 5(3)(a) thereof. The leadership of educational institutions is faced with the stark reality of ensuring that there are gender parities in these institutions as envisaged in the constitution of the republic of Kenya.

> Research shows that the national economic and social costs of not educating girls and not achieving gender parity in education are high; and higher, in fact, for Africa than for any other region (http://www.grida.no/publications/et/ep4/page/2639.aspx).

The UN Secretary General addressed this issue in gender disparity in his keynote address to an overflow audience in Irvine Auditorium on April 4th–5th, 2011. In the final Report of the 5th Global Colloquium of University Presidents, titled *"Empowering Women to change the world: What Universities and UN can Do,"* he stated thus:

> Women remain second-class citizens in too many countries, deprived of basic rights or legitimate opportunities, and he challenged the participants in the Colloquium to help in the fight to overcome discrimination and change perceptions about what women can and should do. (Ki-moon, 2011).

In an interview with Jeff Koinange, K24 TV channel in Kenya, broadcast on on February 14th, 2012, Aicha Bah Diallo, Forum for African Women Educationists (FAWE) Chairperson and Chairperson and Advisor to the Director-General UNESCO on education maintained that women do better in high positions of leadership. She cited the case of Liberia where Ellen Johnson Sirleaf has proved to the world that women are capable of leading their countries if elected to these positions. The question to ask then is what can be done to ensure that the middle level female staff is provided with the adequate resources they need to further their education?

Methodology

The study utilized qualitative approach. Qualitative research expands the range of knowledge and understanding of the world beyond the researchers themselves. It often helps us to see why something is the way it is, rather than just presenting a phenomenon. In our case, thirty female middle level staff members were interviewed using open-ended questions. Those interviewed had worked between five and twenty eight years at the university. They were holders of ordinary level certificates, professional certificates, diplomas and degrees when they were hired at the University. Since then, some had obtained degrees (undergraduate and post graduate), and diplomas in various fields. Many of them had completed computer packages, attended workshops and International Standard Organization (ISO) courses.

I applied and obtained permission to conduct the research from the relevant university administration personnel. All participants signed a consent form that explained the objectives of the research. They were assured confidentiality and anonymity. The study was voluntary and they could withdraw at any time without penalty.

Data Analysis and Results

This study was designed to investigate the level of support for the education of female middle level staff at Moi University. In reviewing the data, a few themes emerged:

a)   low level of education at entry level,
b)   professional development opportunities,
c)   stagnation due to bureaucracy,
d)   lack of clear criteria for promotion, and
e)   minimal financial support to further education.

Low level of education at entry level

Most staff interviewed had worked for between five and twenty eight years. Most of them entered the university with Ordinary Level, Advanced Level and Diploma certificates in various disciplines such as secretarial studies. A few of them entered with first degrees in areas such as home economics, sociology, and computer science. There were those who have gained working knowledge through workshops and ISO training while at the service of Moi University.

Professional development opportunities

A few of the female staff indicated that they had received sponsorship to further their education from the institution. This could be in the form of partial tuition payment or staff development funds. For the most part, most of them pursued higher learning by obtaining government or cooperative society loans. Others used their own savings or borrowed money from family members. Most staff interviewed agreed that Moi University had been able to provide staff development funds that have assisted them to pursue further training and that the university had provided some opportunities for educational growth. Some participants indicated that Moi University was a good institution to work in since there are incentives for those interested in furthering their education. This had helped female staff improve in their abilities for personal success at their various stations of work, both in academic and administrative divisions. Others shared that Moi University had been good for their careers. For the period they worked there, they had gained a lot through professional training. They averred that the institution had provided them with room for training hence opportunity to grow while working. Given that it is a learning institution, they had developed academically. Some had learned many things through experience and their career in various disciplines had improved. The university had made them learn how to work with different kind of people especially male superiors. Further to these, the university had an Institute for Gender, Equity, Research and Development based at the office of Deputy Vice Chancellor Research and extension that had been at the forefront in enabling them to push for the female agenda in areas of recruitment and training of staff.

Stagnation due to bureaucracy

While many of the female staff members interviewed found their work fulfilling, they also indicated that there was a lot of bureaucratic red tape when it came to promotion. This was well summarized by a participant who said: "I have worked for five years without a chance to advance my career because of work being inflexible". One participant shared that "the work has been challenging due to bureaucratic processes that allow decisions to be made after a long time".

There are also challenges working at Moi University. Female staff have had to go through the monotony of working in same offices for a long time, for example, working in one office/department for more than ten years without transfer and/or promotion as one participant shared: "I have worked in the same office for more than ten years without a transfer or promotion". Their professional growth was delayed due to bureaucratic processes that allowed decisions to be made after a long time without involving them. Some had worked for five years without a chance to advance their career because of work being inflexible. Those who work in academic divisions had more challenges especially because promotions take a long time to come even after acquiring the required degrees.

Lack of clear criteria for promotion

Many of those interviewed felt that the institution was not doing enough to recognize those who had achieved higher education since hiring. There was no scheme of service to help them get into a higher job grade automatically after obtaining the required credentials. This made some think that promotion was not on merit as was well-summarized by one participant: "People should be promoted and placed in the right place once they attain certificates. Hard work should be recognized and its benefits should be enjoyed by the university".

There was also a general feeling that when vacancies came up, the institution did not assess the available skills appropriately before advertising to the general public. As such the result was low rate of promotion even after attaining new levels of education. This sentiment was expressed by a participant who stated thus: "Do not employ external candidates when those in the system can adequately provide the same service, recognize your own and make them proud to be of service to the system."

A few of the female staff received salary increments after they obtained a higher level of education. One participant was given a two-year salary increment after she published a journal article and presented a paper at an international conference. One participant was given a promotion to a middle level position after graduation with diploma. However, the promotion was not instant even after the certificates were deposited with the relevant bodies. It took one participant seven years to get her promotion while another took five years.

Minimal financial support to further education

Some staff benefited through sponsorship by Moi University. In many cases this was partial sponsorship under staff development, which they supplemented with bank and cooperative society loans. Some even used personal savings. Full government sponsorship was rare, they said. They overcame some of the financial needs through seeking funds from Higher Education Loans Board (HELB).

In general study arrangements were challenging. A majority of them managed to complete their studies through great sacrifices, especially in the financial aspect, taking classes over weekends and after work on week days. Looking for resources as well as delegating their office duties was some of the other challenges faced. Scheduling time management well to suit their time of studies posed a big challenge. In addition to these, pressure of work and shortage of staff in most departments meant that they had to stay around and do most of the routine office work.

Discussion and Conclusion

While it is true that furthering of education for female middle level staff at Moi University must also be motivated by the need for the same by these staff cadre, the university as an institution must seek to enhance their chances for promotion to senior staff by supporting their education financially. The cost of living and factors of inflation in the country do not leave many staff with the capacity to develop themselves academically. Their education levels will go a long way in setting the stage for cadre succession in case of retirement and other causes of attrition. The university has training programs for staff, but the main problem is that the amount of money allocated is usually insufficient. In this respect, the university needs to allocate more funds for female middle level staff rather than leave them to compete with their male counterparts for the little annual allocations.

But at Moi University, reward through promotion is never guaranteed and is never attached to one's new level of education. Few female middle level staff got promoted after successfully completing their education. Some were only given salary increments which were so little to them compared to time and resources they spent in acquiring their new level of education. And yet some of them were academically competent and contributed to journals and even presented papers both locally and internationally. Those who were lucky to be promoted got the promotion after a long period of waiting.

Some got their diplomas and later decided to pursue various degrees to enhance their knowledge and experience. Some registered for Masters degrees despite the fact that they had not been promoted previously. Acquisition of further education is presumed to help the said employee deliver her work satisfactorily, unfortunately these rewards have not been forthcoming. The university only recognized them after a long time through letters of recognition. Those who participated in conferences abroad had their air ticket paid for plus room and board. Some were given only certificates of participation.

Given that they work at an institution where education of higher learning is offered, members of staff can attend classes and be at their place of work. Knowledge is power hence educated women are empowered. An educated employee takes instructions easily with less supervision. Whatever area of study undertaken by these middle level female staff, it should be done for the mutual benefit of both the university and these employees. Most of them met criteria for furthering their studies. The studies give them the opportunity to disseminate the knowledge to schools, churches and to educate the community in which they live in. As females, they could easily understand the problems facing female child especially when they are in a higher position of authority. They need further education due to global development and the changing technology. The training of female staff is important to them because of career progression and to bring new ideas into the system, to boost self-esteem. Through education they will improve on their profession because they have what it takes to further their education. Also, to achieve organizational goals and development of their careers, as one participant shared "we are in a developing world and technology is changing for better services".

These middle level female members of staff believed that further training would make them exercise team work; enable people air their views freely. They preferred democratic and participatory approach to service delivery and good governance. Customer satisfaction and quality service have lately become very vital in most of the corporate organizations and institutions of learning such as the university. Participatory and democratic approaches to governance give people freedom to carry out their job as they understand them without fear of coercion and bureaucracy. They also encourage innovation thus improving performance. The only goal for the employees is to promote the mission, vision and core values of the university charter even after the attainment of new academic status.

Way Forward

Moi University should provide Opportunities for female middle level staff to pursue graduate and first-professional degrees in designated fields where women traditionally have been underrepresented at the university and where the employment outlook and earnings potential are strong. It should set up Career Development Grants for female middle level staff to support those who hold a bachelor's degree and are preparing to advance in their careers at work place. Special consideration is given to female middle level staff since they are the next tier of staff after the senior staff. They should be assisted to publish their research. Women in various segments of society including Moi University require support for the enhancement of their education already covered by career development grants.

Moi University should partner with other organizations such as FAWE which work hand-in-hand with communities, schools, civil society, Non-Governmental Organizations and ministries in assisting female middle level staff. Their work influence government policy, build public awareness, demonstrate best educational practice through effective models, and encourage the adoption of these models by governments and institutions of education.

References

Chelala C. and Manuel P. (2009). Education Helps Break Cycle of Poverty. Retrieved from http://www.theepochtimes.com

Christine R. M. Kiganda (2009) Governance Challenges of the 21st Century in the East African   Universities Keynote Speech for the Annual General Meeting of the Inter-University Council for E. Africa.

Citizen TV, 9.00 PM News Bulletin, 19th February 2012.

Coleman, I. (2010). Women Are Transforming the Middle East. Random House. Retrieved from www.cfr.org › Women Fourth World Conference on Women, Beijing, China 4-15 September 1995.

Constitution of Kenya (2010). Government Printer, Nairobi, Kenya.

Hannan, C.(2005) UN's Division for the Advancement of Women. *Africa Renewal.* Vol.19 page 6

Heathfield, S.M. (2006). "Employee Management and Leadership in the Workplace. *Innovative Approaches to Employer Engagement in Further Education,* Research Paper 1 p.6.

Ki-moon, B. (2011). Final Report of the 5th Global Colloquium of University Presidents. Retrieved from http://www.upenn.edu/president/global_colloquium/outcomes-

Merton, R.K. (1968) *Social Theory and Social Structure*. New York: Free Press.

Mulili B. M. (2011) Corporate Governance Practices in Developing Countries: The Case for   Kenya. *International   Journal   of Business Administration* Vol. 2, No. 1; p.17

Njogu, K. & Orchardson-Mazrui, E. (2006) Gender Inequality and Women's Rights in The Great Lakes: Can Culture Contribute To Women's Empowerment? Retrieved from http://www.unesco. org/new/fileadmin/MULTIMEDIA/HQ/SHS/pdf/Culture-Womens-Empowerment.pdf on July 23, 2013

Turnbull S. (1997) *Corporate Governance: An International Review*, Blackwood, Oxford, vol. 5, no. 4, (pp. 180-205).

United Nations Education, Scientific and Cultural Organization (UNESCO) (2000). World Education Forum in Dakar, Senegal, April 26-28, 2000. http://unesco.org.

SECTION THREE

HEALTH RELATED ISSUES

CHAPTER 8

MOTHERS' KNOWLEDGE ON VACCINE PREVENTABLE CHILDHOOD DISEASES: A QUALITATIVE STUDY OF MOTHERS WITH CHILDREN UNDER FIVE YEARS OF AGE IN UASHIN GISHU COUNTY OF KENYA

Theresah Wambui

Immunization remains one of the most important public health interventions and cost-effective strategies to reduce both morbidity and mortality associated with infectious diseases (Odusanya, Alufohai, Meurice, & Ahonkhai, 2008). According to Adenyinka (2009), immunization is estimated to save at least 3 million lives from vaccine preventable diseases. Despite this, vaccine preventable diseases remain the most common causes of childhood mortality with estimated three million global deaths each year mainly in Africa and Asia, among children less than 5 years old (Centre for Global Development, 2005). Uptake of vaccination services is dependent not only on provision of these services, but also on other factors including knowledge and attitude of mothers (Mtsumura, Nakayama,Okamoto & Ito (2005); Torun & Bakirci (2006). In 2009, an estimated 82% of children globally had received at least three doses of DPT1 vaccine (DPT3) (WHO, 2010). Additional vaccines have now been added to the original six recommended in 1974 (WHO, 2010). Most countries, including the majority of low-income countries have added hepatitis B and Heamophilus influenza type b (Hib) to their routine infant immunization schedules. As well, an increasing number are in the process of adding pneumococcal conjugate vaccine and rotavirus to their schedules (WHO, 2010). Worldwide studies report that successful immunization of children depends on mothers' existing knowledge and positive attitude that is supported by aspects of the socio environment including beliefs about infectious disease threats, ideas of the social responsibility, and high levels of declared trust in

1 DPT (also DTP and DTwP) refers to a class of combination vaccines against three infectious diseases in humans: diphtheria, pertussis (whooping cough), and tetanus. The vaccine components include diphtheria and tetanus toxoids and killed whole cells of the organism that causes pertussis (wP) (Wikepedia).

authorities, a willingness to conform and a strong sense of societal responsibility.

A study by Benin, Wisler-Scher, Colson, Shapiro & Holmboe (2006) found that trust or lack of trust in relationships were main determinants of mothers' decisions about vaccination and that this reliance on trust was especially impressive, because mothers perceived that "diseases are not around" or "is not so bad" and that they had little experience with vaccine-preventable diseases. The social status of women was recognized as playing an important role in accessing immunization services. While the responsibility of immunization was left totally to the mother, the socially subordinate role of women did not provide the means of getting the immunization services. A study carried out in the United States determined that for mothers with multiple children, less education, and low incomes had a higher risk of having under-vaccinated children (Luman, McCauley, Shefer & Chu, 2003). Mothers from a range of socioeconomic and educational backgrounds would understand and appreciate the social nature of vaccination decision (Leask, Chapman, Hawe & Burges (2006), but in rural communities mothers are not empowered with education and belong to lower socioeconomic status and therefore pay less attention towards child health.

A mother's knowledge, attitude and practice play a major role in achieving complete immunization before first birthday of the child. The majority of rural women are illiterate, have low education and belong to low-income group (Nisar, Mirza & Qadri, 2010). They have vague knowledge related to vaccine names, the timing of the immunization (Impicciatore, Bosetti, Schiavid, Pandolfini & Bonati, 2000) and are often not aware of diseases in Expanded Programme on Immunization (EPI) programme. According to Tadesse, Deribew, Woldie & Mirkuzie, (2009), a significant proportion of children (42%) in their study did not complete the recommended immunization schedule. The drop-out rate was higher compared to a study conducted in Kenya which recorded 22.6% (Ndiritu, Cowgill, Ismail, Chiphatsi, Kamau, 2006). Sign & Yaday, 2000 also found that mothers had fair knowledge regarding the need for immunization, but had poor knowledge regarding the diseases that it prevents. Mothers' lack of knowledge on vaccine preventable diseases was associated with no or delayed immunization. A study in Rajasthan found that specific information about vaccine preventable diseases other than polio was very limited in mothers (Manjunath, Pareek, 2003).

In the past, African countries have experienced high infant mortality rates due to many infectious diseases. However, over the past several years the vaccination of targeted child population has reduced these deaths, thus making this intervention the highest priority for the authorities (Fourn, Haddad, Fournier & Gansey, 2009). Childhood immunization represents the gateway to provision of comprehensive health care to which all children ought to be entitled. Vaccinations are cost-effective with respect to life years saved (Rwashana, Williams, & Neema, 2009).

In Kenya, the proportion of children aged 12-23 months that reported to have received all recommended vaccinations is 77.4%. However, this proportion varies from 48.3% in the North Eastern Province to 85.8% in Central province (Kenya National Bureau of Statistics (KNBS) 2009). This study therefore explored the knowledge domain of mothers in relation to vaccine associated with preventable diseases.

Methods

Setting: The study was carried out within the peri-urban areas in Uasin Gishu County of Kenya. The peri-urban areas are mostly composed of a socio-economically disadvantaged population with a largely menial work income. In the selected areas the primary level health care services are offered at the health centres. Two health centres within the peri-urban areas were selected for the study. These centres provide clinical services, immunization and maternal and child health services to the community members.

Participants: Study participants were mothers of child bearing age (15-49) who had at least one child under the age of five, and attending one of the selected health facilities either for child immunization or other health services. The age of those interviewed raged from 18 to 38 years. Most of them had only primary school level of education and were mainly stay at home mothers. The number of children the women had ranged from one child to six children. All the women had at least one child younger than five years eligible for vaccination.

Research instruments: Focus group discussions and in-depth interviews were utilized for data collection. A semi-structured interview guide was developed within the light of the existing literature. The interview guide explored the mothers' knowledge of immunization: the importance of immunization, the sources of immunization information, the number of times a child should be taken for immunization, the circumstances why children miss some immunization, the decision-making process and how to ensure all children receive proper immunization

Procedure: Permission to conduct the research in the two centres was sought from the Medical Officer of Health of a municipality within Uasin Gishu County. The cooperation of the staff at the health facilities was also sought through the nursing officer in-charge. Two researchers and four fourth-year nursing students visited the two health centres (A and B) for formal introduction. After giving a brief description of the purpose of their visit they invited the mothers who had children younger than five years old to participate in the study. The mothers were given an informed consent form which assured them that confidentiality and anonymity would be maintained at all times. The study was voluntary and they could withdraw from the study at any time. Participants for focus group interviews were recruited from the immunization area where they presented their children to be immunized.

Seven guided focus group interviews with the eligible mothers present at the health centres were conducted. These were four focus group interviews in health centre A and three in health centre B. Each focus group consisted of 15 participants. A total of 105 participants participated in the focus group interviews. A total of 60 participants for health centre A and 45 participants for health centre B. The focus group interviews lasted for one and a half to two hours. The participants were asked to give their oral consent for audio taping the discussion. As one researcher facilitated the discussion, the other researcher took notes and the four nursing students were observers. After the focus group discussion, there were in-depth individual interviews for mothers who had come with their under-five year old children to the health centre for other health services. Mothers for in-depth interviews were recruited from the outpatient department where they had come with their under-five year old children to receive other health services. The purpose of the research was explained in a clear and simple way and those mothers who consented were interviewed after the provision of health services. A total of 42 mothers were interviewed.

Data analysis

The focus group as well as the in-depth interviews were conducted in Kiswahili. These were then translated into English by one of the researcher who is a proficient speaker of Kiswahili. The focus group and in-depth interviews were transcribed verbatim. Transcripts were read several times and the key themes were identified and coding frame developed. The comments of the mothers were referenced with the generated themes. The two researchers who were involved with coding process exchanged the coded material to ensure reliability.

Results

From the transcripts, a number of themes emerged as follows;

a) the mothers' perception of immunization;
b) sources of information regarding immunization;
c) number of times a child needs to be taken for vaccination;
d) the knowledge concerning the names of the vaccine preventable diseases;
e) reasons why children miss certain immunizations, and
f) interventional strategies that would enhance proper immunization.

The mothers' perceptions of immunization

The mothers' participating in the study did not know the definition of immunization but portrayed their perception of immunization as being of great importance because it protects their children from getting the childhood infectious diseases that could cause disability and even death. They considered immunization as a life saver as shared by one mother: "immunization is important because when a child is immunized, he becomes healthy and is protected from diseases. I do not want my child to be handicapped. ("Sitaki mtoto wangu awe kiwete", loosely translated to mean "I don't want my child to be disabled"). Some mothers believe that immunization would boost the child's immune system and thus it would reduce the number of times the child would be taken to the hospital due to disease and this reduces the costs of going to the hospital. Others said that when a child is immunized if he contracts a disease like measles, it will not be very serious as shared by one mother: "When my child is immunized and gets measles, during an outbreak, the disease will not be serious as it would be if not immunized." Other mothers bring their children for immunization because they were told to bring the child to the clinic during delivery as shared by this mother: "I was told during delivery to bring this child to the clinic and that is why I am here."

Sources of information regarding immunization

The mothers had obtained immunization information from various sources. Some reported to have obtained the information from the media, particularly broadcast media (radio and television). Other mothers got the information during antenatal clinic attendance and from the hospital during delivery. Others claimed to have obtained the information while in school and some were informed by their parents as they were growing up as one mother said: "I got the information from the hospital when I was coming for clinic and also heard from my parents when I was growing up. Other places are media, mostly radio."

Number of times a child needs to be taken for vaccination

This was something that the mothers did not know. The number of times varied greatly and some of the mothers were not sure of the number of times they needed to bring their children to the clinic. Some talked of three times, others four times, five times and one mother said she did not know the number of times but a rough guess was six times. Others said it was monthly for nine months. They were just guessing. Other mothers talked of where the child was injected when they brought the child to the clinic as one mother shared:

I took my children to the clinic for immunization five times each. After birth, they received an injection on the hand and some drops on the mouth, then an injection on the thigh for three times and the last one at nine months on the hand again. (A mother in health centre A)

Mothers had their children's immunization cards. Howevery, they could not even go by the card and say how often they are supposed to bring their children to the clinic. Some said that the nurses always tell them when to bring their children to the clinic and that they write the dates on the immunization book.

The knowledge concerning the names of the vaccine preventable diseases

The mothers were aware of the diseases that are preventable by vaccines and were able to name some of the diseases like polio, measles, tuberclosis (TB), whooping cough and pneumonia. They said that these are the diseases that are usually emphasized as one mother said: "I know a number of diseases like polio. The government always emphasizes more on measles and polio. Recently I heard that they introduced a vaccine against pneumonia". Other participants also gave names of non-immunizable diseases like marasmus, kwashiorkor and malaria. A few mothers said they did not know the diseases because when they come to the clinic they are never told what diseases the vaccines prevent. The mothers also did not know which vaccine was administered to their children. This is because they usually do not read the vaccine from the vaccination cards and they could not get satisfactory information from the health personnel administering the vaccine as one mother shared: "You cannot understand it [which vaccine was administered] from the card; also the health personnel do not say anything. You just take the child and they give the vaccine."

Although some of the mothers stated that they wanted to know which vaccine was administered, they were inhibited by the negative attitude portrayed by the health personnel as shared by another mother: "We do not even know which vaccine is administered to our child; we cannot ask as we do not have the courage to ask."

Reasons why children miss certain immunizations

The participants reported that a child would miss immunization due to various reasons. Some indicated that this would be due to their religious beliefs and especially in the rural homes. Majority of the participants cited the mother's ignorance and negligence, lack of money and being too busy as one participant put it:

> I know many women here are not educated and hence ignorance is a contributing factor. Others are lazy and avoid coming to the clinic mainly because of negligence. Some women may be willing to come to clinic but they lack money and sometimes they are too busy especially market days.

What was also reported as reasons was lack of nearby health facility, inadequate vaccines at the clinic and illiteracy. Other participants indicated that mothers are too busy making money and therefore cannot create time to bring their children to the clinic for immunization. Others fail to take children to the clinic due to poor transport, ignorance and religious beliefs as one mother shared: "Default by the mother to take the child to the clinic is due to poor transport if the clinic is far, ignorance and religious beliefs for churches that are against medication".

Participants also shared that nurses are often very harsh and more so if you come on a date other than the one on the card. This makes the mothers afraid and therefore will fail to bring children to the clinic for immunization. A mother may also fail to bring the child to clinic if the child is critically ill or if the mother is ill or is a drunkard. One mother shared the following: "A parent may fail to bring their children for immunization because of drunkenness which will make her to forget things and others due to forgetfulness". Some participants also reported that mothers fear to bring their children mainly because many react to the vaccines and can affect the child's health as one mother said:

> I do not know of any taboo or religion prohibiting immunization but what I have heard is that mothers fear to bring their children mainly because many react to the vaccines. *[Hizo chanjo hufanya mototo awe mgonjwa, kwa hivyo wazazi hususia kuja clinic* - Those vaccines make the child sick, therefore some mothers refuse to bring them to the clinic.]

Interventional strategies that would enhance proper immunization

The participants indicated that there is need to create awareness on the importance of immunizations. They suggested that a door-to-door immunization campaign initiative should be implemented and more clinics opened in the rural areas. One mother had the following to say: "House to house immunization should be done. That is the only solution to this."

Other participants stated that outreach activities to educate mothers should be increased and involve the fathers as well. The majority of them also reported that those out-reach programs should reach all the people in the village so that defaulters can be reached. Most of the participants stated that importance of immunization should be broadcast on the radio and television, and also put on posters as one mother shared: "To ensure that all children receive proper immunization we should broadcast on the radio and television, that it is a must for every child to be brought for immunization and say why it is important to do so."

Some mothers stated that for children to receive proper immunization, people should stop drinking locally brewed alcohol. One mother said: "To ensure that all children receive proper immunization people should stop drinking local alcohol especially in our location because it has ruined a lot of lives." One participant stated that "all parents should be taught the importance of immunization and stern measures taken against parents who fail to have their children immunized".

Discussion & Conclusion

This qualitative study explored the knowledge domain of mothers in relation to vaccines associated with preventable diseases. Although the participants were not able to give a definition of immunization, they had perceived immunization as of importance and therefore of great necessity. The participants were aware that childhood immunization prevents babies from contracting infectious diseases that would otherwise cause death and disability and perceived immunizations as of great benefit and a necessary practice.

Several limitations should be acknowledged in assessing results of this study.

First the researchers had initially planned to conduct focus group discussions but it turned out that focus group discussions (in typical sense) were not possible. This is because with introduction of the topic, all mothers looked down shyly and none of them was ready to initiate the discussion. This resulted into the use of unstructured questionnaire than focus groups discussions.

The second limitation was the timing. The focus group interviews were scheduled after mid-day because the venue for the interviews was the waiting bay of the immunization department. It was not possible to adhere to the ideal number of participants of a focus group interviews (6-8). The number kept on increasing as mothers continued joining in as they found the discussions interesting and the number for each focus group interview was 15 participants.

A third limitation was that participants were recruited from immunization and out-patient waiting rooms. In an indirect way, this may have self–selected participants who have access to health care and who are more motivated to visit health care facilities to get their children immunized. Thus, the results obtained from this small selective sample cannot necessarily be generalized to the sub populations, which likely include mothers who do not visit healthcare facilities on a regular basis.

Finally, although Kiswahili is the country's national language, conducting interviews in Kiswahili could have inhibited some of the participants from being more fully involved because of their perceived low proficiency in Kiswahili.

Despite these constraints we believe that these results are still a valuable contribution to the literature on knowledge status of mothers' in relation to immunization in Kenya. The principle aim of this study was to explore the mothers' knowledge regarding diseases that are vaccine preventable.

The findings concur with studies that have been carried out elsewhere. Knowledge status of the mothers in relation to immunization was found to be poor but their perception was that immunization prevents babies from contracting infectious diseases and babies cannot die from these diseases. According to Topuzoğlu et al. (2007), mothers were aware that childhood diseases could cause disability and death, and they perceived immunization as a beneficial and a necessary practice. This was partly because the experiences about the consequences of the vaccine preventable diseases were still fresh in the minds of these mothers.

There was a believe among the participants that immunization boosts the child's immune system, reducing the number of times the child could be taken to the hospital due to disease and this takes into account the costs of going to the hospital. Immunization could prevent disability and even death because when children are immunized, they do not suffer much when they get an attack by an immunizable disease.

The perception of immunization is perhaps what motivates mothers to take their children for immunization. Jheeta & Newell (2008) reported that the demand for vaccination is triggered by a general perception that vaccines are good for infants and a strong feeling of vulnerability to serious illness. When children are not immunized, they would probably get very sick and might die; therefore mothers would want their babies healthy, and free of incurable disease. Immunization is said to promote the health of the child but not all women perceive immunization as a necessary practice for their children, and so they would only bring their children to the clinic because the decision to do so has already been made by somebody else. Petousis-Harris et al, (2004) and Smailbegovic et al, (2003) reported that women did not refuse vaccination, rather they had a lack of awareness related to the experience of 'not being immunized but still staying healthy,' and it was different from the concerns about safety of immunization which was recognized in the industrialized countries. In our study there was no evidence for outright rejection of immunization by any of the participants but they reported that they have heard of people disapproving of immunization.

Although mothers reported various sources of information about immunization, this study recognizes the lack of effective communication and information transfer between the health personnel and the mothers as an important obstacle for getting services as also cited in other studies (Tarrant & Gregory, 2003); (Streefland, Chowdhury, Ramos-Jimenez 1999); (Streefland, 2001).

It was also determined that mothers' knowledge relating to vaccines preventable diseases and the timing when vaccines should be given was vague. This portrayed some kind of ignorance. They claimed that nurses always told them the return dates. Awodele et al, (2010) showed that most mothers do not know the appropriate time schedule for vaccine administration and the exact time to commence immunization.

Mothers were also not informed which vaccines were administered to their children. Since they lacked effective communication channels with the health care personnel, mothers tried to rationalize the need for immunization from the attitudes of the health care workers. The disapproving attitude of the health care workers when mothers delayed the immunization session by coming late made them to perceive immunization as an important issue. This then highlights a dependent relationship between mothers and healthcare workers which do not provide a ground for effective information transfer. Although the mothers were convinced that immunization is essential for their children, they were hesitant to ask questions or communicate with the health personnel and so they lacked the necessary information (Helman & Yogeswaran, 2004). Namuigi & Ohuanukoonnon (2005) reported that some health workers wrote the dates of the next immunization in the baby's health book and pointed out to the mothers who could read, which was very helpful in reminding the mothers. According to Tarrant & Gregory, (2003), knowing or witnessing childhood deaths and disability from these diseases might have caused a risk perception and motivation to seek immunization for their children among the mothers because they would not want their children to die.

In regards to vaccine preventable diseases, mothers gave the names but also named other diseases that are not vaccine preventable. The incorrect responses is an indication that some mothers still have poor understanding of the concept of immunization and this would go a long way to affect the uptake of immunization. Mothers erroneously believe that immunization prevents HIV/AIDS as well as diarrhea. This may be due to that fact some health educators do not specifically state that not all childhood diseases are vaccine preventable, hence some mothers are left to assume that it confers an all-round protection (Adenyinka, 2009).

The distance from a mother's homes to the health facilities seems to have an important factor affecting immunization: transport costs, loss of time, unfriendliness, and even aggressive responses by health staff towards latecomers all interact to become a strong barrier to future immunization. Fear of rebuke has been reported in other studies as contributing to non-adherence relating to routine clinic attendance (Montgomery, Mwengee, Kong'ong'o, Pool, 2006). Children missed immunization when either the mother or the child is sick. Others are mothers' alcoholism and forgetfulness or they are too busy with other activities especially during the market days. A study by Boffarraj (2011) reports that child sickness as a cough was observed to be the main reason of cessation of immunization followed by social reasons and forgetfulness and these reasons were also found to be similar to other studies by Saunders, (2000) and Impicciatore et al (2003). Also mothers are too busy with their daily chores without leaving any time for them to bring their children to health centres (Namuingi & Phuanukoonnon, 2005). Topuzoğlu et al (2007) stated that in their study, the important barrier to their services related to the economic constraints and accessibility of the services. The study reports that although the immunization services were free of charge transportation needed money or the mothers had to travel long distances to access the services.

For an effective immunization programme, out-reach immunization activities should be instituted with door to door campaign and parents be empowered to freely and clearly express their attitudes towards childhood vaccinations. Jheeta & Newell (2008) stresses that strengthening advocacy, communication and social mobilization will enhance informed and willing participation in vaccination programs. This study underlines a need to make childhood immunization as a 'felt need' of the community. Efforts to increase the knowledge and understanding of the mothers of children who are less than five years of age about the essentiality and benefits of the immunization should be implemented. The health personnel should embark on micro-teaching to mothers before immunization sessions begin. The Kenya government should ensure equitable dissemination of readable materials in relation to immunization in simple, but effective, messages. The health workers should also be equipped with better communication skills and an attitude of care.

Further exploratory study on the impact of communication on benefits of childhood immunization needs to be conducted. This would increase knowledge for mothers of young children on the importance of vaccination to the overall health of their children.

Although the mothers' knowledge on immunization was poor, the general awareness of the diseases was good. Majority of the participants have good perceptions towards immunization. Most of the mothers had their children immunized based on the health care giver and recommendations from other people. To ensure children receive proper and timely immunization, appropriate information need to be disseminated and aggressive campaign on children immunization need to be put in place.

References

Adenyika D. A. (2009). Uptake of childhood immunization among mothers of under-five in Southwest Nigeria. *The Journal of Epidemiology.* V (1)2

Awodele O., Oreagba I. A, Akinyede A.A, Awodele D. F &Dolapo D. C (2010).The Knowledge and attitude towards childhood immunization among mothers attending antenatal clinic in Lagos University Teaching Hospital, Nigeria. *Tanzania Journal of Health Research* V (12) 3

Benin A.L, Wisler-Scher D J., Colson E, Shapiro E.D & Holmboe E.S (2006). Qualitative Analysis of mothers' decision-Making about Vaccines for infants: The Importance of Trust. *Pediatrics* 117; 1532

Bofarraj M. A. M (2011). Knowledge, attitude and practices of mothers regarding immunization of infants and preschool children at Al-Beida City, Libya 2008. *Egypt J. Pediatric Allergy immunology.* 9(1):29-34

Centre for Global Development (2005). Making markets for vaccines: from ideas to actions. Centre for Global Development; Washington DC.

Fourn L., Haddad S., Fournier P. & Gansey R. (2009). Determinants of parents reticence towards vaccination in urban areas in Benin (West Africa). *BMC International Health and Human Rights* 2009, 9 (suppl 1): S 14   doi: 10.1186/1472-698x-9-S1-S14

Helman CG, Yogeswaran P. (2004). Perception of childhood immunization in rural Transkei: A qualitative study.*SAMJ.* 94:835-8

Impicciatore P., Bosetti C., Schiavid S., Pandolfini C., Bonati M. (2000). Mothers as active parents in the prevention of childhood diseases: natural factors related to immunization status of preschool children in Italy. *Preventive Medicine.* 31:49-55

Jheeta, M. & Newell, J. (2008). Childhood vaccination in Africa & Asia: The effects of parents' knowledge and attitudes. *Bulleting of the World Health Organization* v. 86(6): 419

Kenya National Bureau of Statistics (KNBS), ICF Macro (2009). Kenya Demographic and Health Survey 2008-2009.

Krueger, R.A & Casey M.A (2000). Focus Group: A practical Guide for Applied Research, 3rd ed. Sage Publications, Thousand Oaks, CA.

Leask J, Chapman S, Hawe P, Burges M. (2006). What maintains parental support for vaccination when challenged by anti-vaccination messages? A qualitative study. *Vaccine* 24:7238-45.

Luman E T, McCauley MM, Shefer A, Chu SY (2003). Maternal characteristics associated with vaccination of young children. *Pediatrics.* 111 (5part 2): 1215-18

Matsumura T., Nakayama T., Okamoto S., Ito H. (2005). Measles vaccine coverage and factors related to uncompleted vaccination among 18-month-old children in Kyoto, Japan. *BMC Public Health, 2005,* 5:59

Manjunath U., Pareek R.P. (2003). Maternal knowledge and perceptions about the routine immunization programme-a study in a semi urban area in Rajasthan. *Indian Journal of Medical Sciences.* 2003; 57:158-63. [PubMed]

Montgomery C.M., Mwengee W., Kong'ong'o M., Pool R. (2006). 'To help them is to educate them': power and pedagogy in the prevention and treatment of malaria in Tanzania. *Tropical Medicine & International Health.* 11(11 November):1661-9.

Namuigi P. & Phuanukoonnan S. (2005). Barriers to measles immunization: the beliefs and attitudes of caregivers in Goroka, Eastern Highlands Province, Papua New Guinea. *Papua New Guinea Medical Journal.* 48:3-4

Ndiritu M., CowgillKaren D., Ismail A.,Chiphatsi S., Kamau T.(2006). Immunization coverage and risk factors for failure to immunize within the Expanded Programme on Immunization in Kenya after introduction of new Haemophilus influenza type b and hepatitis b virus antigens. *BMC Public Health 2006,* 6: 132.

Nisar N., Mirza M., Qadri M. H. (2010). Knowledge, attitude and Practices of Mothers regarding immunization of one year old child at Mawatch Goth, Kemari Town, Karachi. *Pakistan Journal of Medical Sciences.* v (26) 1 Retrieved from: www.pjms.com.pk

Odusanya OO,Alufohai EF, Meurice F P, ahonkhai V,(2008). Determinants of Vaccine Coverage in Rural Nigeria. *BMC Public Health.* 8:381 doi: 1186/1471-2458-8-381

Pertousis-Harris H, Goodyear-Smith F, Turner N, Soe B. (2004). Barrier to childhood immunization. *Vaccines.* 22:2340-4

Rwashana A.S., Williams D.W., Neema S. (2009). System dynamic approach to immunization in Healthcare issues in developing countries: a case of Uganda. *Health Informatics Journal.* 15(2):95-107

Saunders N. (2005). Maternal knowledge, attitude and practices concerning child health care among mothers of children younger than 60 months in Kep District, Kingdom of Comodia. University of Toronto, Faculty of Health. *Center for International Health;* 1:2-30

Singh P, Yadav RJ. (2000). Immunization status of children of India. *Indian pediatric.* 37:1194-9

Smailbegovic M. S, Laing G, J, Bedford H. (2003). Why do parents decide against immunization? The effect health beliefs and professionals. *Child Care Health Dev.* 29:303-11.

Streefland P, Chowdhury AMR, Ramos-Jimenez P. (199). Patterns of vaccination acceptance. *Social Science Medicine.* 49:1705-16

Sreefland P, (2001). Public doughts about vaccination safety and resistance against vaccination. *Health Policy.* 55: 159-72

Tarrant M, Gregory D. (2003). Exploring childhood immunization uptake with First Nations mothers in north-west Ontario, Canada. *J Advanced Nursing:* 41:63-72.

Topuzoğlu A., Ay P., Hidiroglu, S. &Gurbuz, Y. (2007). The Barriers against childhood immunization: a qualitative research among socio-economically disadvantaged mothers. *The European Journal of Public Health.* 17 (4): 348-352

Torun SD, Bakari N (2006). Vaccination coverage and reasons for non-vaccination in a district of Istanbul. *BMC Public Health.* 6: 125

World Health Organization[WHO] (2010). Immunization service delivery ad accelerated disease control. Expanded Programme on immunization Retrieved from http//www.who.int/immunization_ delivery_en/ on: 3/19/2011

SECTION FOUR

OTHER EDUCATION ISSUES

CHAPTER 9

ROLE OF FATHERS IN THE HEALTH AND WELLNESS OF THEIR CHILDREN

Caroline Sawe

Introduction and Background

Addressing father and male involvement in parenting is not an easy task. On almost every indicator of child well-being, children today fare worse than their counterparts did just a generation ago (National Child Welfare Center for Family Centered Practice, 2002). The reason proposed by some is the dramatic rise, over the last 30 years, in the number of children living in fatherless households (National Child Welfare Center for Family Centered Practice, 2002). Recent research has shown that fathers have an important contribution to make in many aspects of their children's well-being (Rosenberg & Bradford, 2006).

Historically and culturally, there is still a widespread and deep belief that mothers should be the principal parent, and that there is something wrong and odd about men who are strongly pulled into the nurturing role. Children development studies has focused more on the sensitivity of mothers towards fulfilling their needs. However, there is need to focus on the fathers' roles and attitudes in the fulfillment of children's needs (American Psychological Association, 2013).

There is an African proverb which states that "it takes a village to raise a child" and with all the fragmentations in the modern society the "village" that raises these children is at best a village of two. Modern fathers tend to be more involved in care giving than protecting, promoting and improving the health and well-being of their wives, newborns, children and adolescence directly (Allen & Daly, 2007).

It is important to know that the influence of a father's love on child's development is as great as the influence of the mother's love. A father's love helps children develop a sense of place in the world, which helps their social, emotional and cognitive development and functioning. Moreover, children who receive more love from their fathers are less likely to struggle with behavioral or substance abuse problems (Allen & Daly, 2007). Research has also shown that fathers who are more involved in their family issues, feel better about themselves, their wives feel better and their children become more popular and successful in their education (Allen & Daly, 2007).

Modern fathers are no longer the traditional breadwinners and disciplinarians in their families. They are more than capable caregivers to families and they too face the daily physical and psychological challenges like mothers do. Psychological research across families from most ethnic backgrounds and in urban setup show that fathers' affection and increased family involvement has really helped promote children's social and emotional development (Lerner, Noh, and Wilson, 1998). In most recent decades the changing economic role of women has greatly impacted the role of fathers. Due to an increased number of working age women, employed or looking for job at an earlier age, harder economic times and more financial assistance needed in a family, there is need for fathers to be involved in parenting fully including involvement in their children's healthcare (Lerner, Noh, and Wilson, 1998). Men have not been involved in some family issues because of many factors including culture, economy and busy schedules.

Yet research shows that children growing up without fathers are more likely to fail in school or to drop out, engage in early sexual activity, develop drug and alcohol problems, and experience or perpetrate violence (Allen & Daly, 2007). A good father is critical to the optimal development and well-being of a child. A father's role is more than that of economic provider and includes nurturing, caregiving, and emotional support in both obvious and subtle ways. Successful fatherhood correlates strongly with many attributes of children successfully growing up. This includes physical and mental health habits, success in school, self-respect and self-esteem, respect for others and for appropriate authority, constructive social and peer activities, as well as the avoidance of substance abuse, delinquency, and other forms of high-risk behaviors (Allen & Daly, 2007).

Programs to help men be better fathers, understand their roles and responsibilities of rearing a child, learn about child development, find out alternative disciplinary options, and, in some cases, how to be a man, are emerging nationwide. There are many reasons why fathers and men are "missing" when it comes to child welfare (Rosenberg & Bradford, 2006). These reasons are magnified within the distressed circumstances that are characteristic of the child welfare population. To address this absence of fathers, with the goal of creating greater accountability and responsibility on all sides, we need to begin with this cornerstone fact: fathers and men are excluded within the policy, programs, and practice of child welfare (Rosenberg & Bradford, 2006).

Literature Review

Fathers are playing an increasingly larger role in childcare, and health care providers must include and educate fathers as key players in their children's health, rather than focusing on mothers only. A study done in Northwestern University Feinberg School of Medicine reported that lower-income Chicago urban fathers were involved in their children's health and encouraged them to exercise and eat healthy foods (Paul, 2011). But these same fathers may have also given their children the wrong dose of medicine and they may be uncomfortable handling emergency medical care for their children (Paul, 2011).

Recent research has shown that a vast majority of fathers will attend the birth of their children whether or not the men are married to the mother (Allen & Daly, 2007). Research goes further to say they really are involved day-to-day with their children in ways that affect their health and development (Allen & Daly, 2007). The number of stay-at-home fathers in the United States has nearly doubled to 158,000 from 2003 to 2009, and the number of single fathers raising children has grown from 400,000 in 1970 to 1.7 million in 2009, according to the U.S. Bureau of Census (Paul, 2011). But when it came to navigating an emergency room with his daughter, a dad named Dante said the situation was scary, because he was used to his wife handling things (Paul, 2011). Another dad admitted giving his daughter soda and cookies, although he knew he shouldn't.

> In pediatrics we play lip service to fathers being involved, but we could do a better job of working with them. They come with the best of intentions, but don't know what they should be doing. From the first visit with a newborn in the nursery to a checkup with a teenager, health care providers can encourage fathers and show them ways to positively interact with their children. (Garfield as cited in Paul, 2011, par 16)

In a Longitudinal Studies of Child Abuse and Neglect (LONGSCAN) consortium in 2002, Dubowitz and colleagues examined fathers' effects on the functioning of 677 six-year-olds. The children rated support from their fathers or father figures in terms of companionship, emotional support, practical support, and tangible support. Children who reported stronger father figure support felt more competent and socially accepted and had fewer depressive symptoms. Non-biological father figures had just as positive an influence on the children as did biological fathers. Father support did not affect children's externalizing behavior problems or cognitive development (Dubowitz, Papas, Black, & Starr, 2002). The study also supported the idea that father involvement benefits children. Based on this evidence, child welfare workers should encourage positive interaction and support between fathers (including father figures) and their children. There are many reasons why fathers and men are "missing" when it comes to child welfare. These reasons are magnified within the distressed circumstances that are characteristic of the child welfare population (Dubowitz, Papas, Black, & Starr, 2002).

Father involvement requires understanding and transitions. Many fathers have difficulty sustaining emotional ties and social commitments when they experience risk factors such as substance abuse, poverty, mental health issues, and unemployment (National Child Welfare Center for Family Centered Practice, 2002). To keep them involved requires understanding and emphasizing life transitions. Fathers need to be given opportunities to understand the changing roles that accompany major milestones such as pregnancy, birth, and rearing a child. Increasing their ability to provide familiar, stable, daily routines will help create important resources in a child's life. Fathers' participation during birthdays, holidays, school graduations, and other rituals are the building blocks of their engagement (National Child Welfare Center for Family Centered Practice, 2002).

In a study done in Johannesburg, South Africa, men were asked if they thought it was "good" or "not good" to accompany their wife to Ante Natal Clinic (ANC) and to provide a reason for their opinion (Mullick, Kunene and Wanjiru, 2005). More than two-thirds of the men (67.9%) responded that it was good to go to ANC visits with their wives. One hundred and nine (43.3%) said that they had accompanied their wife at least one time. Only those men responding positively identified that they had ever accompanied their wife. The proportion of men accompanying their wife increased as age increased. The 171 men who said it was good to go to ANC with their wife were asked to give their reasons. Forty-nine (28.7%) identified that accompanying the woman would help the man learn and increase their knowledge of ANC activities; 33 (19.3%) said that this would show true love and keep the woman happy; (36.3%) men who thought it good but had not gone to ANC, 34 (54.8%) said that their work would not allow time, which was compounded by the long waiting time in the clinic. Twelve men were supportive but said that tradition was not conducive to going to ANC. Sixteen men provided no reason. Seventy-seven (30.6%) men responded it was "not good" to go to ANC, 16 (20.8%) said it was not their custom to participate in ANC; 14.3% said it would be shameful to accompany the wife to ANC; and 10 (13.0%) said there would be no one to care for the home. Seven (9.1%) men gave no reason for this opinion (Mullick, Kunene and Wanjiru, 2005). There is no doubt that fathers' involvement in their children's well-being is beneficial in many ways. However, there are barriers that continue to hinder fathers from active involvement. How can these barriers be broken?

Methodology

Study Area

The study was carried out at Moi University Dispensary in Uasin Gishu County, Kenya. The University has approximately 3,000 male staff.

Sampling

The study population were male and fathers working at the University. A total of nine fathers were interviewed and observations were done at the University dispensary Mother Child Health (MCH) department. Purposive sampling and snowball techniques were employed in the research.

Participants

Nine fathers participated in the study. Two of them were recruited at the dispensary MCH department. The youngest was aged below twenty five years and the rest ranged between 26 and 45 years old. All the selected fathers signed a consent form and volunteered to participate in the study. This is a brief description of each of the participants. Pseudonyms were used to ensure confidentiality and anonymity.

Jese: Holds an undergraduate degree and is a father of one. He is 25 years old. He got his first born child in the year 2009 and he really felt good. He did not feel well at the hospital when his wife had gone to deliver. He said the last time he checked the immunization records of his child was six months earlier and he has never accompanied his child and wife to the clinic though he says he has once talked to a health care worker regarding his child's well-being. He agreed that it is important for fathers to be

115

involved in the well-being of their children but culture and lack of time are some of the main barriers to his direct participation in his child's well-being.

Mos: Holds a diploma and has six children. He has been a father since 1994. He built a house so as to improve their economic status when they were expecting their first child. He accompanied his wife to the hospital and he felt very well while there. He checked the immunization records two years earlier and he agrees that it is important to accompany his wife and children to clinics but culture and economic hardship are the main barriers to this.

Joj: Holds an undergraduate degree and a father of one child born in 2011. He said he gathered all the things his wife needed for the baby. Though he accompanied the wife to the hospital, he said that he was very embarrassed at the hospital. A year earlier was the last time he went through the child's immunization card but he agrees too that it is important to be involved in the well-being of their children. Male ego and culture does not allow him to be involved directly. Joj was below 25 years old.

Coll: Holds an undergraduate degree, had six children and was a first time father in 1991. He did nothing in preparation for fatherhood. He did not accompany his wife to hospital for delivery. He has neither accompanied his wife or children to the clinic and the last time he checked the immunization card was the date of immunization. He said that it is the woman's role in knowing and tracking the well-being of children

Mak: Holds Doctor of Philosophy, has three children and was a first time father in 2009. He had saved some money in preparation for fatherhood. He accompanied his wife to hospital for delivery and he was afraid while in the hospital. He has accompanied his wife and children to the clinic and the last time he checked the immunization card was a month prior to the study. Job commitments are what are making him not to be involved in the well-being of his children and wife.

Nell: Holds a master's degree and had three children. He really felt good when he had all his children and he did not accompany his wife to hospital for delivery. He could not remember the last time he checked the immunization records though he has been reminding his wife to be checking the records. He said that it is the woman's role in knowing and tracking the well-being of children. He said that fathers should really be involved in the well-being of their children

Amro: Holds an undergraduate degree and had one child who was born in the year 2009. He felt good when the baby was born and he had saved some money and helped in buying the baby's supplies. He did not feel well when he accompanied his wife to the hospital. He frequently checks the immunization records but he has never accompanied his wife and child to clinic. Culture and work commitments are some of the major barriers to his involvement, but he accepts and agrees that fathers need to be involved directly in the well-being of their children. He suggested that policies on paternity leave need to be reviewed and enforced by the government; hospitals and doctors need to come up with programs like open air clinics that will be targeting fathers and men.

Kaoz: Holds an undergraduate degree and a father of three children. He agreed that being involved in children's well-being is important. He said he had never accompanied his child to clinic but he had for his wife. He was 36 years old.

Mol: Holds a master's degree and a father of six children since 1998. He felt nice when he had his first child in the year 1998. He had saved money in preparation for fatherhood. He too agreed that it is important for fathers to be involved in the well-being of their children.

Instruments

Questionnaire: Ten item interview schedules were administered to the nine participants and were thoroughly probed by the researcher. The first participant led the research team to the next participant who also led the researcher to the next participant until the target number was met. It targeted nine questions specifically on involvement of the father on the well-being of both their wives and children. It also targeted the fathers who had accompanied their wives and or children to the MCH clinic.

Observation: Observation method was also used to collect the data. The researcher was based at Moi University Dispensary MCH department room and observed the following and recorded them accordingly: the number of fathers who had accompanied mothers and or children to the clinic, healthcare providers and whether they were encouraging mothers to bring the fathers of their children to the clinic.

Document Analysis: Posters of the walls of MCH, brochures, magazines or any reading material on the display desk were analyzed for father-friendly messages.

Procedure: Permission was sought and granted by an administrator at the MCH to conduct the study. All the 9 participants were given an informed consent form containing information regarding the purpose of the study, specifically what can be done to encourage fathers to be more proactive in terms of their children's early health and the benefits of study to the target population. The participants were also informed that data would be collected by use of questionnaires and interviews. They were guaranteed confidentiality as each participant was identified with an anonymous number and not by their names or personal file numbers. They could withdraw from the study at any time without penalty because it was voluntary.

Results

Demographic data

Out of the nine participants, five were aged between 26 and 35 years old, three were aged between 36 and 45 years and only one was aged below 25 years. Five of them had undergraduate degree as the highest level of education, two were holders of Masters Degree while one had a diploma and one was a holder of a doctorate degree. Seven of the fathers had more than one child while the other two had one child each. Seven of them had had other children while two had not had other children.

First time fathers and preparation for fatherhood

Participants were asked the year they had their first child, how they felt the first time they became fathers, what they had done in preparation for fatherhood, if they accompanied their wives to the hospital when they were going to deliver and how it went while in the hospital. Three of the participants had their first babies in the year 2009, one in the year 1991, one in the year 1993, one in the year 1994 and one in the year 2011. One did not give the year. All the nine participants were very happy and excited the day they became first time fathers. One said that it was a wonderful and great experience the day he saw his first baby. Five of the fathers had saved some money in preparation for the new born, two of them helped their wives in gathering baby's supplies like clothing, diapers, and organized for transport for the mother to the hospital. Some of the fathers prepared as they waited for their first born child. One said that he build a house so as to enhance their economic well-being. A few bought the baby's necessities in advance like clothing, food and so forth. Only one father said he did nothing in preparation for fatherhood. Seven of the fathers accompanied their wives to the hospital while two did not accompany them. Five of them felt excited and good while in the hospital, one felt very embarrassed, two did not feel well and were also afraid and one father felt that the situation in the hospital strengthened their marriage. The one who felt embarrassed said 'it was fine despite some embarrassments' Four of them felt that the other children (2nd, 3rd etc. born) brought more understanding in their marriage.

Role of fathers in child health and wellness

Asked what their role was in their child's immunization, if they have ever taken their children for immunization, if they have ever accompanied their wives with children to clinics if they usually talk to health care providers whenever they are in clinics and wanted to know the last time they checked immunization records for their children. All the fathers agreed that immunization is very important to children at a young age and they really require their fathers' attention. Four of the respondents said their role in immunization was to provide support like transport and finance to the mother and her child, three said that they always remind the mother of the immunization dates and two said that they always read the records to know how the child is doing in terms of immunization. One said that he kept checking the record of the hospitals thoroughly; another said that he has been reminding the mother to be checking the immunization records frequently. Six of the fathers have accompanied their wives and children to the clinics while three have never accompanied them. Six have talked to the healthcare providers regarding the well-being of either their children or wives or both. Three of the fathers last checked immunization records of their children two years earlier, one checked one year earlier, another checked six months back, another one year earlier, another checks frequently yet one said that he could not remember the last time he had checked the records. Fathers were asked if it was important to be involved in the well-being of their children. All the nine participants agreed that it is very important to be actively involved in the health of their children and their wives.

4

Barriers to involvement in the children health and wellness for fathers

Fathers were asked if there were any barriers to them being involved in the well-being of their children. Five of the respondents said they could not accompany their children and wives to the clinic because culture and beliefs do not allow them to. Some of them said 'cultural beliefs and norms', two of them said that they were very committed at work and therefore did not have time and the other two said that it is the role of a woman to take care of a child's well-being. Some of the responses included; 'that's her role (on other duties)', 'it is the attitude that men perceive as a responsibility of the mother to attend to the child's clinic exercise', 'it is the duty of mothers to take care of the growing child to a certain age before primary education', two said that their ego and chauvinism does not allow them to accompany child and mother to the clinics.

Discussion and Conclusions

Role of fathers in child health and wellness

The purpose of this study was to find out the role of fathers in the health and wellness of their children. The study took place at a university dispensary unit. Scheduled questionnaires and observation method were used in data collection. The results showed that fathers are usually happy and excited whenever they get children and they would like to be involved in the wellness and the health of their children and wives. They are no longer the traditional breadwinners and disciplinarians in their families, but also capable caregivers. This was shown in the study when a number of them were really prepared for fatherhood by saving some money and helping in gathering the basic supplies for newborns. Some even had to build houses so as to cut bills so that they can economically better themselves especially with the presence a new baby.

Most fathers in this study indicated that they had accompanied the mothers to hospital for delivery. This finding concurred with Lerner et al (1998) that showed that majority of fathers were attending the birth of their children whether or not the men are married to the mother. Though the study was done in America where cultural beliefs on who is to bring up children is no longer a major issue, the African culture is being challenged especially on the role of fathers in the upbringing of children. Due to hard economic times and need for more financial assistance, women have been forced to look for employment and this change has impacted the role of fathers in a family. This was shown in the study when fathers have really been checking on the immunization cards frequently and always reminding the mothers on the immunization dates. Some have even been accompanying their families to clinics apart from providing other supports like transport and finances. Eight fathers in this study said that they had accompanied their wives to antenatal clinic which is higher compared to a study that was done in South Africa which showed that only 43.3% had ever accompanied their wives to clinic (Mullick, Kunene and Wanjiru, 2005). The rise in number might have been attributed to educational background and the waiting time in the clinics where each client was served for less than ten minutes. Fathers in this study agreed that it was important to be fully involved in the well-being of their children as supported in the study by Dubowitz et al (2002) that fathers' love help children develop a sense of place in the world which helps their social, emotional and cognitive development and functioning.

Barriers to involvement on the children health and wellness for fathers

Culture, beliefs and norms proved to be the main barriers to fathers and their children well-being. A study done by Allen & Daly (2007) showed that fathers who wished to be involved with the care of their children regardless of financial and marital status were marginalized and overlooked. This is in line with this study because some men felt that it was against their culture and belief to be involved directly with a child's health and especially when they are still young. Their ego and pride could not also allow them as they felt that it was the responsibility of their wives. Busy work schedules have also not allowed them to participate. Materials and how the MCH room had also been designed adds barriers to their going to clinics. Reading materials were not father friendly and therefore the government especially the ministry of health should try including messages targeting fathers and other male family members.

The study concluded that it is important for fathers to be involved fully in the wellness and health of their children and their wives. It is important for them to be accompanying their family members to clinics and they should also appreciate the fact that even women go through the same daily physical and psychological challenges that they do go through. It is important for policy makers to review policies on child upbringing and wellness. There is need to create awareness on the role of fathers in the wellness and health of their children. More research should be conducted on the role of modern fathers in different cultural settings especially in rural Kenya.

References

Allen, S. & Daly K. (2007). The effects of father involvement: an updated research summary of the evidence inventory. University of Guelph, On. CA: Father Involvement Alliance (FIRA) © Centre for Families, Work & Well-Being. Retrieved on July 23, 2013 from http://fira.ca/cms/documents/29/Effects_of_Father_involvement.pdf

American Psychological Association (2013). The changing role of the modern day father. Retrieved on July 23, 2013 from http://www.apa.org/pi/families/resources/changing-father.aspx

Dubowitz, H., Kim, J., Black, M.M., Weisbart, C., Semiatin, J., & Magder, L.S. (In press). Identifying children at high risk of child maltreatment. *Child Abuse and Neglect.*

Dubowitz, H., Papas, M. A., Black, M. M., & Starr, R. H. Jr., (2002). Child neglect: Outcomes in high- risk urban preschoolers. *Pediatrics,* 109(6), 1100-1107.

Lerner, R., Noh, R. & Wilson, C. (1998). The parenting of adolescents and adolescents as parents: a developmental contextual perspective. Retrieved on July 23, 2013 from http://parenthood.library.wisc.edu/Lerner/Lerner.html

Mullick, S., Kunene & Wanjiru, M. (2005). Involving men in maternity care: health service delivery issues. *Agenda Special Focus.* Retrieved on July 23, 2013 fromhttp://www.popcouncil.org/pdfs/frontiers/journals/Agenda_Mullick05.pdf

National Child Welfare Center for Family Centered Practice, (2002). Father involvement in child welfare: Estrangement and Reconciliation. Retrieved on July 23, 2013 from http://www.hunter.cuny.edu/socwork/nrcfcpp/downloads/newsletter/BPNPSummer02.pdf

Paul, M. (2011). Lower income dads active in their kids' health: dads encourage exercise, healthy diet but may give wrong dose of medicine. Retrieved on July 23, 2013 from http://www.northwestern.edu/newscenter/stories/2011/10/garfield-low-income-dads.html

Rosenberg, J. & Bradford, W. (2006). The importance of fathers in the healthy development of children. Office on Child Abuse and Neglect, U.S. Children's Bureau. Reconciliation. Retrieved on July 23, 2013 from https://www.childwelfare.gov/pubs/usermanuals/fatherhood/chaptertwo.cfm

CHAPTER 10

INCEST: BREAKING THE SILENCE ON GIRLS' ISSUES OF SEXUALITY IN SECONDARY SCHOOLS IN KENYA

Kamara Margaret Kosgey

Introduction and Background

Incest, defined as an intimate sexual relationship among relatives, is a taboo subject which is rarely discussed or acknowledged in many communities (Kamara, 2011). This has been the woe of the girls who are often the victims. It was during a prior research encounter on the challenges that teen mothers face in secondary schools, that I first got insight into the prevalence of incest, a sexual taboo in the traditional African culture (Kamara, 2011). A desperate need to share with the researcher the pain of being branded as immoral and the desire to be understood in the context of teen pregnancy actually led to the revelations of the girls' sexual vulnerability within the home and family environment (Kamara, 2011). Mothers had exposed the daughters to sexual pests in the name of relatives: uncles, cousins, brothers, fathers and other relations as dictated by the African kinship structures (Datta, 1984). The girls revealed that in their mothers" absence, many of them were left under the care of uncles or bigger brothers who, instead of offering security, ended up turning to prey on the girls in such vulnerable circumstances. Other girls claimed that their own friends had been sexually abused by fathers in the absence of mothers during domestic rows and separation.

Incest, in the traditional African culture, is a sexual act that would have warranted a cleansing ritual for the offenders lest misfortunes befell the concerned family (personal communication). This only referred to a situation where relatives unknowingly engaged in a marriage (sexual) partnership. And it was especially where children, born out of wedlock would get into sexual relationships with those in the family or people who got married in or to, a family where a close relation was earlier married. Some form of incest was however condoned socially and culturally, being related to African masculinity and cultures. These culturally accepted forms of incest existed in some communities where training youth in sexuality led to demonstrative sexual encounter with close relatives. In a certain community in western Kenya, an aunt would be allowed to have a sexual encounter with nephews to teach them the act of sexual intercourse to enhance sexual intimacy and prevent marriage failure (personal communication). Others engaged in activities like wife inheritance by sons of a father who happened to leave behind a young wife, and inheritance by cousins or brothers (Nyakwaka, 2005).

What I found most striking though, during the entire research, was that great difficulties involving incest were worsened by multiple communication barriers and constraints that inhibited exposure of the problems and made incest a taboo topic. This is despite the silent pain that is often endured by girl victims of incest. Ironically, the few girls who had sought to share their pain after incest were hushed and threatened to silence by mothers and other confidants to keep it secret. One can only guess the reason for such threats: it was either to conceal the shameful family experience or to protect the male ego of the offenders. Such might appear as a special and rare case of experience in school, yet how many other girls might have the same difficulties out there? How many more serious pertinent issues related to incest remain uncommunicated and therefore unattended to in schools and society? What are the long term effects of such hidden knowledge and pain? These were questions that drove me to engage in this research. As I set out to work, my key purpose of this study was to investigate the existence and experience of incest among secondary school girls. It is hoped that the taboo surrounding the content and context of incest will be broken and in future, open discussions and debates will eventually see the practice of incest and the traumatizing effects of incest brought into control.

Theoretical framework and Review of Literature

This study was informed by the liberal feminist theorists who seek to investigate the essence of the existing gender exclusion of girls in all spheres of life (Patton 2002). Specifically, the liberal feminists concentrate on discovering inequalities in the provision for education for women, and establishing and protecting equal opportunities for women through legislation and other democratic avenues such as research, public awareness campaigns and mobilization of stakeholders (Patton 2002) in critical gender issues. Such an avenue can be the creation of awareness on the reality that is incest, and one that can be of use in ensuring action against the practice of incest while creating democratic avenues that can be used to deal with the vice. The theory also advocates for support groups that should in this case assist to rehabilitate such traumatized incest victims and enhance their education provision while sensitizing the girls to fight incest. Liberal feminists seek to work through existing systems to bring about reforms in a gradual way (Patton 2002). The purpose of this study therefore was to find avenues of addressing the plight of girl victims of incestuous relationships. Further, the study was intended to find out what can be done to lessen the impact of such trauma on their education, especially secondary school education. Working through the system would involve the classroom activities, general social discussions and counselling to identify the challenges that girls undergo and seek workable solutions towards incest.

Incest; a taboo that is in crisis

Research in matters of sexuality reveals that many problems that emanate from sexuality, like incest, occur because many youths and adolescents do not know how to handle their sexuality (Lips, 2008). The same argument is echoed by Oluruntoba-Oju (2010) who argues that the role of cultures in prohibiting discussion about sexuality especially for children is responsible for the many evils that come with it. Children grow up knowing that sexual excitation or issues of abuse are best unspoken because presumably, both the culprit and the victim are already guilty of delving into the world of adulthood. Worse still they had broken the sacred role of reproduction, the presumed role sexuality was meant to play in the majority of African cultures. As put by some scholars, this situation was under control so long as the cultural norms and traditions were intact (Ruto, 2007). Ironically, the sexuality prohibits are expected to be restrictive of the same people whose lifestyles have been greatly changed by westernization leaving a knowledge and practice vacuum that breeds this anti-social approach to sex and sexual fulfillment. Unable to handle the instinctive sexual drives and to express them openly, victims opt to hide and secretly engage sexually with the closest person with least suspicion or threat - the vulnerable family members.

Incest and girls sexuality

A recent study on teen pregnancy found that a number of the teen pregnancies were as a result of incest (Kamara, 2012). Through interviews and focus group discussions the preliminary findings reflected that teen mothers' challenges included incest as a major issue affecting them and other friends who had confided in them.

This research is however limited in the degree to which it addresses incest because Kamara (2012) concentrates on general challenges for teen mothers in school and steers clear of any discussion on incest. The strength of it though, lies in the fact that it is the girls' voice that is heard and the information is not sought for but voluntarily offered implying that it is a major issue of concern to them. This makes credible the incest issues that they raised.

Other research has also shown that in various domestic contexts sex between relations and kin members is rampant and an issue of concern because it is hardly discussed or exposed. Adeli (2011) features incest as a horrifying experience of sexual encounter of girls with brothers and other kin. The study, undertaken by Adeli (2011) on sibling incest involved a survey of girls during a teen camp. The study revealed that a majority of the girls in the camp had been subjected to incest by older brothers. The population comprised of girls from various regions of Kenya who offered firsthand information about sex between siblings. While some cases in the research were reported as resulting from coercion, the shocking reality was that many cases involved consensual sexual encounter that only turned nasty when individuals grew into awareness of incest but found themselves entrapped in it. They got haunted by the fact that it was prohibited in society and it was a taboo culturally, yet they enjoyed it and maintained the practice despite the guilt and trauma that came with it. Adeli (2010) failed to unearth, identify and discuss these sexuality issues and did not reach out to the men and boys who are key participants in the process of incest.

Counseling of incest victims

An old saying has it that 'a problem shared is a problem halved', implying that communication of an issue is crucial to the process of either solving the issue or reducing the impact it causes. It is this lack of channels of communication that this research presupposes as responsible for the continued persistence of girls' sexuality challenges related to incest. This is as portrayed by one such a girl during an interview session with the researcher (Kamara, 2011).

Jenny (not real name), reacting to a question as to whether guidance and counseling departments in schools handled their problems effectively, had the following observation to make: *that the victims find it difficult to share such experience because it is not only embarrassing, but people might as well never believe them.* The victims forego counseling despite their troubles. One such victim confided how she was repeatedly abused sexually by her maternal uncle and that the baby whose father's identity she had hidden all along was actually her uncle's. This basically exposes great weaknesses in the communication of the girls' inner conflicts and pain to the people who should provide relieve in shared difficulties and provide for them protection or legal intervention in more serious cases. This causes major constraints in girls' education despite the availability of guidance and counseling in schools and defeats the very purpose of the government policies that should ensure education for all, through the gender equity endeavour (MOEST, 2005; MOEST, 2007). What can be done (a) to open up channels of communication for victims of incest as well as (b) the lessen the impact on the girls' learning?

Research Design and Methodology

Research design

The research took the grounded theory research design developed by Glaser and Strauss in the 1960s. Using the phenomenological approach, the study views incest as a phenomenon of interest to the researcher, not as an abstract area of study but as one that is grounded or rooted in observation and participation of both participants and the researcher as a participant observer. A passage on incest was to be used as ground for discussions through which new insights would be generated. In such a grounded theory design, the researcher uses participant observer research method. The research seeks to understand the respondents understanding of phenomena and takes it as truth. They see the informant as insider expert and during the research they use the informant as folk model telling stories of experience.

The grounded theory takes the form of field research to study things as they are. It begins with raising of generative questions which help to guide the research. Such open questions are, however, not confining but enhance data collection as a lengthy process whose data at times surpasses the said question. Co-concepts are seen developing around the main concept in the course of data collection.

Research setting

The study took the form of a case study of a co-educational high school in Kenya where I taught and where I could work with students as a participant observer. During the study, I sought information from both boys and girls in forms three and four, generally within age sixteen to nineteen. I presupposed that at that age, they were well out of the shy stage that could inhibit discussion on incest. Another reason was the fact that the sexuality theme in the school's curriculum that deals with child abuse and issues like rape and sexual exploitation fall in the forms three and four syllabuses hence settling the ethical considerations that would have been a barrier in the lower classes. I sought to establish what students in the institution knew about incest as guided by some discussion questions, a phenomenon common in a case study (Fraenkel & Wallen, 2000; and Patton, 2002). The study also was meant to extend to the school teacher counselor whose first encounter during discussion of ethical issues already reflected lack of discussion of incest in the department. As a result, there was no need for further interview for the teacher. Such is the situation reflected by the ground theory that sometimes the data collection through group sessions leads to increased insight as new observations lead to new linkages of the research process which in turn necessitates revision of both method and/or data. I was particularly interested in the students' attitudes, opinions and knowledge of incest and the impact it has on girls' education from the grounded approach of the ideas and issues raised in earlier research (Adeli, 2011).

Sampling

All the students, from third and fourth forms were purposively selected to participate in the class focus discussion while the teacher counselor was interviewed. All the students in forms three and four participated in writing an essay with incest as a theme. After the sessions, volunteer students who made comments or carried the discussion beyond the classroom with reference to the discussion on incest were also considered as crucial participants. Given in the context of a class assignment, the underlying obligation to contribute fully in class ensured rich and valid information. It also provided participants a chance to understand the topic in the context of the comprensive passage through peer assistance and expert intervention by the teacher. This paved way for a rich discussion during the next stage of the data collection when deeper understanding and clarifications from individual students was sought through the contributions of key participants. In the next stage of data collection, an essay topic was issued where students wrote an essay each on their views and opinions of incest in their background experiences. In the context of the essay writing, individual concerns regarding the topic were addressed by individual students.

Instruments

A comprehension passage adapted from a research paper on incest was used with open ended questions. The compiled essays were used to identify, name, describe and categorize data on the phenomenon of incest. Such a process allows for open coding in data collection, where every textual paragraph is read in search of an answer to certain questions like those about incest. The passage was edited to remove phrases that may influence the responses of the respondents. The passage, adapted from Adeli (2011) on sibling incest and set with open ended questions, sought to asses understanding of incest from the point of view of students as in: do they understand what incest is and what is the context of incest in the given passage as compared to their childhood experiences and knowledge? In what forms does incest exist? Is it a persistent problem? What did they think about it?

This is the essence of the grounded theory's phenomenological approaches in the data collection.

Field notes were also used to record observations within the discussion or outside as part of journal notes of the researcher's ideas and observations.

Procedure and ethical considerations

Before the actual research, there was a session held with the teacher responsible for counselling over ethical concerns. The teacher, as a specialist observed that since it was within the realms of child abuse, a course theme designed by the Ministry of Education to expose learners to forms of child abuse, the incest topic was not only appropriate but also educative. She later mentioned the same to the parents during the fourth form parents meeting, eliciting support from parents. Being a regular class activity, the sensitivity of the topic was also not inhibitive and the taboo that would have hindered discussion of the topic elsewhere was dealt with in the introduction in each session during the research.

I first arranged to make copies of the passage enough for each student participant. I showed a copy to the teacher responsible for counselling who confirmed that the research would not cause any possible harm to the students as it was thematically within the areas covered in the stipulated curriculum in the study of English and the research site was also at a teen girls camp, a group within the experiences of the students.

Prior to the lesson, adjustment was made to accommodate an 80-minutes lesson for the third and fourth form streams, respectively. The process took two syllabus weeks. During the lesson planning for the form four, five minutes were allocated to the introduction to the lesson structure and content, five minutes for reading the passage, thirty minutes for the group discussion, thirty minutes for the group presentations and ten minutes for the class secretary's round up of the discussion and the teacher's review.

The passage on incest which had been produced earlier and a copy issued to each student during the lesson meant for study skills. As a participant observer researcher, I kept field notes on the students' reaction, comments, gestures and body language as integral and crucial sources of data an aspect of the grounded theory as in Strauss and Cobin (1990), and in Borgattis, (2006). It takes the form of literary analysis, keeping journals and memos and field notes in the process of data collection. Observation is not only tied to textual information as from the group discussions and reports but it is also the behaviour displayed, the reactions, verbal and nonverbal and the interaction of students during such class engagement during the research (Borgattis, 2006).

A proficient reader was appointed to read the passage loudly to the class. I highlighted the main issues pertaining to the passage. I explained that just like rape, which had been featured in the class text two weeks earlier, incest was a related topic that involves child abuse. I made it clear though that the lesson findings would be used to generate research data which may lead to publication. I also made it clear that just like the research sources of other research findings shared with them earlier, their identity would not feature as a school and as individuals and they had the right to decline to take part in the discussions if they so wished. I then explained to the class their rights to avoid the discussion if, in any way, it made them uncomfortable. I used the chance again to brief them on informed consent in research and ethical concerns that protect the research participants from possible harm. The core interests of the research were also mentioned at this point.

Focus discussion groups based on class activities grouping were formed just like in normal class activities. A group secretary volunteered in each group to take down the group findings. In the groups of four, and guided by the formulated open ended questions on the comprehension passage, the class discussed the context and content of the passage while the class secretaries recorded the responses.

The secretaries then reported in turns the findings of each group to the class from what they had compiled as the class clarified issues that were not illustrated. The purpose here was to allow the class to own the research. Once reported, I identified the main issues that came up, those that were common and those that were unique and the peculiar ones that may have needed clarification later.

According to Trochin (2006), the grounded theory focuses on people's subjective experiences and interpretations of the world: how the world appears to others. The rest of the week was devoted to impromptu discussions, observations and consultations that came up as a result of the class discussion. This is because, qualitative research is continuous and gets definitely demarcated when the researcher decides to quit (Trochin, 2006) by which time; he/she has a clear picture of the phenomenon of interest. The discussion actually generated a hot debate over the lunch break and a group from a different class visited my office for a discussion.

During the second week, and also as a measure of reliability of the data I got in fourth form, I gave the third form a composition to write individually during a single forty minutes lesson. During the lesson, students were assigned an essay entitled 'incest' to be written in between 350-450 words, just like in normal class activities in composition writing. I explained that the essay was not going to be awarded marks because it was meant to be a forum for expressing opinion based on knowledge, research and personal experience of incest away from fiction. The class had earlier learnt about *Expressing facts and opinion as opposed to fiction, a study skill covered during the language classes* and they could distinguish the difference in such writing. The purpose was to ensure that students did not just write for marks and scores and in the process fake information, but also to see if the findings in fourth form were any different when compared to the third form who wrote to express themselves prior to the open discussion in class. I collected the essays for assessment.

During another eighty minutes session, the form three classes were involved in a discussion like the previous one for the fourth form. There was however not much in the introduction since they were already familiar with the topic. A group secretary volunteered in each group to take down the group findings. The secretaries then reported in turns the findings of each group to the class as the class secretary compiled the reports. The class secretary then reported the findings as the class clarified issues that were not well illustrated.

Data Analysis and Findings

Data analysis involved textual data, and nonverbal communication analysis through both open coding from the field notes, memos and the essays and selective coding of the data from the discussion. Code notes were generated and used to categorize data into thematic categories derived from the research questions generated from the passage and the essay. On receiving the passage, students were excited and the first reading was accompanied with interjections that reflected that it was not a new topic. A boy who normally sat silent and almost petrified would later in the discussion narrate a horrifying encounter with incest at a neighbour's house. There was remarkable difficulty in self-expression when students narrated such painful encounters about incest that they had heard from friends.

In reviewing the data, a number of themes emerged:

a) Incest as fact not fiction;

b) Nature and cause of incest;

c) Restriction and confinement;

d) Domestic violence;

e) Effects of incest on the youth.

Incest as fact not fiction

The findings showed that students were well aware of the existence of incest. Some of the most recurrent issues surrounding the first research question associated incest with early childhood play, intimacy and caressing, restriction and confinement, mental instability, drugs and substance abuse and pornography. Father-daughter incest was associated with domestic violence and family disintegration. Some other less recurrent ones included urbanization and anonymity, cultural erosion and generation gap which were implied rather than mentioned directly. The effects of incest surrounded guilt, poor performance, shame and withdrawal and other forms of mal-adjustment that were implied in some of the descriptions of incest victims' experiences. There was a clear indication that incest was a fact and not fiction to the respondents. There was a unanimous agreement that incest existed and it is rife in the community. Expressions such as *"I totally agree with the author that incest is rampant..." "I agree with Adeli on incest because it is widespread..." "We fully agree with the author that incest exists..."* were repeated by almost all the participants. Evident during discussions was more willingness of girls to contribute to the discussion. During the presentations, it was clear also that there were more narratives on incest than a normal session could accommodate and some of them had to just be mentioned. Even after the class sessions, students kept engaging in the topic whenever we met outside class sometimes to complete their story.

Nature and causes of incest

A girl presenter, probably in defense of girls added that sexual coercion through enticing presents or company was a point of weakness for girls to give in to incest for the victims would automatically trust the offenders who are likely to take advantage of them sexually. During the group presentations and discussions, the class secretary recorded the causes of incest, some of which were then presented. Others were derived from shared experiences. These include normal childhood copying of grownups' chores and responsibilities that stretches to activities of intimacy and sex. Some students told of a few cases of young people who could not give up the incest-related intimacy. This, one student narrated, was something she had witnessed with a first cousin. It had caused traumatic family conflict when it was discovered. Narrating such an experience, a girl used a local dialect to bring out a naughty view of such incest much to the amusement of students to express the magnitude of this child play. Students talked simultaneously each with a story or a fill up to the story being told. In fact, one student said aloud, *'Kama ni hio, kila mtu alifanya' meaning if such play was incest, then many were already involved.* Intimacy and caressing came out as part and parcel of the prolonged association of siblings and close kin that set precedent to sibling sexual encounter.

Though based on the local setting where parental and sibling intimacy does not involve fondling and caressing, there was an observation that blending the urban life with rural life disorientated people. Being a new experience, boys and men are easily turned on if a girl relative sat on their lap and stroke them even if it is out of sheer innocent fondness. Girls from the local setting find themselves in the same situation if they find themselves in the hands of an urban relative who has grown up to accept caressing and fondling as normal between relatives. Generally, arousal will lead into sexual encounter especially if the environment offers secrecy and time for extended intimacy.

Restriction and confinement

Modern lifestyles have led into modern housing with isolated compounds within which children must remain when parents are absent. This prolonged isolation was reported to be a major contributor to the growth of intimacy especially if one of those involved has had a problem that warranted intimate consolation. Moving close to each other, sometimes hurdled together in loneliness or out of fear of foes and darkness, could lead into development of dependency and sexual attraction to each other as a result of proximity, the youths claimed. Pornography and sexual graffiti were also mentioned as occasioning sexual arousal that may result in incest as the observers seek fulfillment or get to practice what they see. This was associated with lengthy parental absence and lack of monitoring of media programs watched by siblings. In fact one boy in third form claimed that a boy from Nairobi had confided how he hated a sister with passion for having rued him into sex during a porno feature that they had sneaked in the house during their parents' absence. Such confinement was also associated to some extent with lack of awareness. Students mentioned accidental incest as common where brothers and sisters developed sexual attraction unaware that they were related. In the African context, siring babies and not taking responsibility has been a common practice. As a result, mothers have been left to look after children as single parents while the fathers settle in with other women and start new families. Filial attraction may bring such siblings together and may eventually be misinterpreted as sexual attraction or love. At another level of awareness mental instability, drugs and substance abuse all reflect a kind of impaired awareness, either natural or induced. Three cases of incest were cited as having been as a result of children with mental challenges like autism and Down's syndrome. Despite their challenges, it has been proved, their sexuality aspect of life is like any other. So, when aroused they go for anybody available for sex, including relatives. Therefore, when they innocently and instinctively get into incest it can be blamed on their mental challenges. Another group of those challenged mentally are the ones on drugs. Their impaired rational thinking leads to such sexual behaviour. A sad and emotional story was one of a father who had infected his wife and four daughters with HIV. The class presenter, who happened to be neighbours to the said family, claimed that the issue had raised a public outcry and people had talked of more such villains in the same village. This behaviour was, reportedly, due to excessive alcohol and a new drug that men were taking to feel high.

Domestic strife

Domestic violence, family break up and/or separation have also been factors. In instances of domestic violence, four cases of incest involving fathers were mentioned. It was reported that quarrels and fights often drove women out of their homes leaving husbands to prey on their daughters. With a kind of sneer on his face, one boy described an ugly encounter of a father who came home to be served by his daughter after sending away his wife and later turned to sexually abusing the helpless daughter. Added to the fact that the majority of violent husbands are also alcoholic, sexual molestation may go on unheeded.

Effects of incest on youth

Shame and withdrawal: Though students who had gone through the experience of incest could not share their feelings directly, some few reports indicated deep sharing with victims who had gone through the pain and torture of incestuous relationships. The worst experience shared was the shame that the victim suffered especially if the act were discovered and/or publicized. With nowhere to hide for shame, students claimed that victims had avoided the public as much as possible, some being unable to visit relatives for years due to shame. One student Bell (not real name) said thus:

> I believe the experience causes shame....I mean one feels... like ...mm... one is known what they do because... like the friend I told you who told me about her father and that thing of sex. Do you know she died "akiflash" (while carrying out an abortion?). You see, she never talked to people or even left the compound. People said her mother insulted her throughout that she run after men. I still believe what people said at her burial that her father "alimpatia hio ball" (made her pregnant).

Though shared by a second party, the pain of such an experience is felt even in the difficulty with which the speaker tells his narrative. Related to shame and withdrawal are issues like abortion and suicide that are reactions to intense stress and trauma, especially when one cannot open up to talk about embarrassing experiences.

Poor performance: Emotional torture, fear and guilt over long periods have been associated with poor performance. A teen mother exposed how three girls who had shared their incestuous encounters had claimed that thinking about what they had done was distractive and it had interfered with their performance in class. One of the girls who happened to be in the same class with another relative found it hard to trust all the boys in his company and it had inhibited her performance in group discussions.

Violence and family disintegration: In situations where incest is discovered, bitterness and the pain of betrayal were reportedly the worst experiences. The case of Bell above is an indication of pain and frustration of betrayal by a father who abuses her and a mother who treats her as the villain accusing her of running after men. The assumption (the daughter's interpretation) is that she runs after the father. It may go without saying that in the background looms a more intense hatred towards such a daughter especially within a society ruled largely by African masculinity that exonerates men from blame in sexual scandals and demonizes women as enticing the men. Siblings who had engaged in incest had been observed to have deep rooted hatred for offending siblings as Gest (not real name) observed.

> I told you people...this incest has more effects than you can imagine. Take for example this girl I told you about. For six years we were together ...every day she is against the step brother and her brother even when they have done nothing. Like in class she was hurt by a nail and next day her brothers are screaming (beaten?). None of them had hurt her. In fact by standard six I was fed up and refused her company. Do you know what she revealed? The two boys had sexually abused her for long time when a cousin showed them those things. They had hidden a broken bottle in the fence to punish her with if she reported. I think she had wanted them to suffer like herself. Even now there are problems there [in that home].

In a case like this, the feelings of intense pain result in violence where the sufferer may inflict pain to himself/herself and even others as a form of projection. Further sharing about Gest revealed that she has the violence tendency even in secondary school and copes with no one at home.

Abortion: Abortion was mentioned a few times where one was carried out by the parents of the girl on learning that she had conceived from a cousin where their mothers were sisters. In traditional African culture, the birth of such a baby in the family would imply that an abomination had been committed and a curse would befall the whole family. Two girls were reported to have sought advice on how to terminate pregnancies arising from sexual encounters with relatives.

Discussion and Conclusion

Factors like cultural erosion and generational gap that result from deviation from traditional African culture have meant that traditional sanctions against culprits are not enforceable. For instance incest villains and victims would no longer be excommunicated from the community, a penalty that previously acted as deterrent to such behaviour. With the social generational gap widening and added to the lack of fear of excommunication and other harsh penalties, youths engage in sex with relatives. With loss of value for taboos revolving around kinship, observers silently condone incest and seek intervention into the repercussions of the act later. It might appears to be a purely Kenyan or even Africa experience, but various literature presents it as a global issue. In the findings of this research, urbanization and anonymity were also blamed for creating a sense of freelance and carefree attitude that encouraged young people to engage in sex even though they are fully aware of their kinship.

Furthermore, with cultural erosion, young people are no longer scared of curses, abominations and taboos that restricted sex and inhibited sexual offenders. In urban areas, the fact that no one cares about what the other does was cited as a contributing factor. As Adeli (2011) puts it, consensual incest between brothers and sisters begins as mild sexual play and as exploration with one another only to grow into a trap of emotional engagement that leaves the young people ashamed and disturbed when awareness grows.

There was a general agreement that sexual intercourse is the most common form of incest, but the students quite often drifted to other related issues away from the main focus of the discussion. In fact one of them clarified that fondling and touching of erotic areas was never taken seriously or regarded as incest. As one student observed, "if you were to take fondling as incestuous you will find a multitude of offenders because many youths have accepted it so long as one did not go all the way".

Other reports in the presentations indicated that the majority of youths are contented with sending sweet and suggestive short messages via cell phone, especially to people who are close to them, in this case, the relatives irrespective of their sex. Some few respondents argued that in actual facts, such cell phone messages spell out things that would have been sexual had it not been the lack of proximity to the relations. This is the picture created by Adeli (2011) where girl respondents claimed to have been introduced to sex by their own brothers. The same phenomenon has in past years been mentioned in urban areas where siblings share beds within crowded urban bed sitters as a result of poverty and congestion. Such siblings and relations encounter open sexual encounters among adults and suggestive intimacy that leads to arousal and sex or simple copying of 'grown up games'.

It is clear that intense issues of sexuality like incest are not easily exposed and the depth and scope of knowledge of what goes on in the girls' life in and outside school may be an area that is not clear yet. Communication is greatly influenced by consultations between guardians and teachers over individual girl issues or the girl's personality, whether inhibited or outgoing. In addition, it is dictated by the relationship the girl has with her kin. At another level, girls' issues related to incest can be communicated to the relevant family members or the teacher counselors. The dilemma, however, of what to tell, how much to tell and to whom, often faces the victim. Confidentiality is often an issue that cannot be ignored in communication of incest due to its sensitivity which inhibits free and open sharing. This phenomenon comes out clearly in teen mothers' claims that some of the teen pregnancies were as a result of incest and the sensitivity of it in context does not allow them to share with counselors (Kamara, 2011). The obvious implications are that unless open forums address incest, the practice is bound to continue threatening girls' socialization in schools and eventually affect their performance.

Basically, there are great challenges facing girls that affect their performance in education and in the general performance of various roles in society as highlighted in government reports. Incest is one such challenge that is silently deterring educational development of girls as they battle guilt and trauma during and after incestuous sexual encounters. Previous studies and reports from school surveys show that despite the existence of education-related gender policies, many girls still drop out of school (MOEST 2007) or if they are retained in school, their education is inhibited by other social factors outside or within the school environment. Kenya particularly has been facing unique challenges in the implementation of gender-sensitive policies as well as ensuring that there is no gender bias, stereotypes, discrimination, violence and various forms of gender exclusion. A great attempt has been made at eliminating them from the education system (GOK, 1999 and MOEST 2007) but progress is slow and girls' suffering continues. This is all the reason why incest should be dealt with alongside low enrolment rates for girls in school and their high rate of drop out from school due to factors like discrimination and teenage pregnancy.

From the findings, one may conclude that it is futile to have high walls for security at home if children's wellbeing cannot be guaranteed. Monitoring child development is a crucial responsibility that parents miss through trusting their children's self-direction. Society still values kinship and parents need to put in place mechanisms that accommodate their children's safety and educate them to learn to say no when threatened by sexual predators. The open communication between parents and children that should enhance notice of early indicators of sexual abuse or unhealthy intimacy seem absent in the reported cases. This only highlights the fact that the problem will continue unabated.

If by the time of this research, incest as a topic had never been discussed earlier for all the students in the two classes, chances are that the phenomenon is replica in numerous other institutions just as it is evidently not a topic in the sex education curriculum in schools. One can deduce therefore that a link of failure in dealing with incest begins at home, extends to the school and culminates into the lack of effective policy and practice regarding sex education by curriculum developers and the Ministry of Education.

The moral fibre that previously controlled traditional African society has also been replaced by modern legal systems that involve presentation of tangible evidence before an offender can be aligned in court. In cases where villains and victims are sometimes willingly offenders, one may never get to know the partakers or to bring to book any offenders.

References

Adeli, S., (2011) Pain or Pleasure; Understanding the Female Experience of Sibling Incest, *Perspective on Selected Critical Gender Issues in Kenya and Beyond* Moi University press, Moi University, Kenya.pp.37-45.

Borgatti, S. (2006) Introduction to Grounded Theory; Goals and Perspective Retrieved from http://www.edu.researchgroundedtheory.analytictech.com

Datta, A., (1984). *Education and Society.* London: Macmillan Educational Books Inc.

Fraenkel, J., Wallen, N. (2000). *How to Design and Evaluate Research in Education. 4th* Edition, McGrawhill Companies, USA.

GOK, MOEST (2007). Gender Policies in Education: Government Printers, Nairobi

GOK, MOEST, (2005). *Policy Framework for Education, Training and Research, Sessional Paper No 1 2005:* Government Printers, Nairobi.

GOK., (1999). *Totally Integrated Quality Education and Training (TIQET), Report of the Commission of Enquiry into the Education System in Kenya*: Government Printers. 1999.

Kamara, M., (2011). Schooling or motherhood; the challenges facing teen mothers in secondary schools in Kenya,in Khamasi et al Eds. *Perspective On Selected Critical Gender Issues In Kenya And Beyond* Moi university press, Moi University, Kenya pp.1-8.

Lips, H. (2008). Sex and gender: an introduction. (6th edition) New York, NY: McGraw-Hil.New York pp 287-288)

Oloruntoba – Oju, T.(1989). The Social and Cultural Construction of Desire and Pleasure. *Sexuality Research,* 26 p. 250-253

Nyakwa, D. A (2005). Gender and sexuality among the Luos of Kenya: Continuity and change. In Khamasi J.W & Maina-Chinkuyu, S. A. (Eds). Sexuality: An African Perspective. Eldoret, Kenya: Moi University Press.

Patton, M. *Qualitative Research and Evaluation Methods*, (3rd edition). Sage publications

Ruto, J.S. (2007). The Toilet Walls Communication in the University: A Private Plea to Address Sexuality Education. *Sexuality in Africa* vol. 4

Trochin, W., (2006). Grounded theory; qualitative approaches web center for social research methods. Retrieved from http://www.socialresearchmethods.net/kb/qualapp.php on March 1, 2012.

CHAPTER 11

TEACHER PREPARATION PROGRAMS IN KENYA: THE CHALLENGE OF FIELD PLACEMENTS

Faith Maina

Introduction

Perhaps the most important part of teacher preparation is field placement. This can be described as that period in teacher preparation programs when student teachers are sent to the field to put the theory they have learned in the college classroom into practice. According to Sigh and Stoloff (2006), "field experiences and clinical practice are considered the most important and most influential component of teacher preparation programs" (p. 1). Field experiences represent "an integral component of teacher preparation programs because they allow teacher candidates to apply and reflect on their content, professional, and pedagogical knowledge, skills as well as dispositions, in a variety of settings" (Sigh and Stoloff, 2006, p. 1). In a study conducted by Gentry (2008) teacher candidates found the most valuable training experiences to be field placements. One participant in the study shared that "she liked field experiences so much because she thinks the only way to really learn something is by doing it" (Gentry, 2008, p. 12).

There are various models that are used by different teacher training programs. Some programs have a one year field placement where student teachers remain in the host school under the supervision of a host teacher, popularly known as the co-operating teacher. In some programs, student teachers are placed in the field for short periods of time and are periodically supervised by the college instructors and regularly by the host teacher. Some are based on close university-school partnerships while in others, the relationship between the placement school and the university is minimal (Sigh and Stoloff, 2006).

In the republic of Kenya, field placement or teaching practice (TP) for Teacher Training Colleges (TTC) is prescribed through a Ministry of Education (MOE) government syllabus especially for the middle level colleges. For primary teacher education (PTE) programs, student teachers are supposed to be placed in the field for three weeks during their first year of training and six weeks during their second year of training. During the time the student teachers are in the field, they are supervised directly by their college instructors who also have the responsibility to approve all their teaching material. During the second field placement, a sample of the student teachers is assessed by an official from the ministry of education.

This study investigated the effectiveness of one field placement in terms of developing quality effective teachers. Quality teacher preparation is a key ingredient in developing skilled human resources crucial to harnessing other endowments that will drive development. Countries around the world are investing in teacher preparatory programs 'with the goal of developing teachers who are reflective analytic practitioners' (Schwab, Defranco & McGivney-Burelle, 2004 p. 21).

Literature Review

Namunga & Otunga (2012) argue that teachers are important components of education whose services are important in the realization of educational goals: "Due to their central role in the enterprise of education, teachers at all levels require effective and sufficient education to be able to adequately carry out their roles and responsibilities" (pg.228). Recognizing that teachers are an important group of professionals who impact virtually on every sector of the economy, "teacher education is considered as an indispensable driver for economic development" (Namunga & Otunga, 2012, p.233). This argument concurs with Schwab et al (2004), who argue that "effective teacher preparation programs could prepare teachers to meet the demands and high standards necessary to prepare students to become productive citizens of the 21st century" (2004 p. 24). In reviewing the literature for effective field placements and clinical experiences for teacher preparation, a number of themes emerged, namely:

a)   Length and variety of field placement;
b)   Student teacher dispositions;
c)   Collaboration and feedback from cooperating teachers and
d)   Reflection and problem solving opportunities.

Length and variety of field placements

How long the student teachers remain in the field matters. A study done by Floyd & Bodur (2005) found that pre-service teachers with longer clinical experiences "were better able to see different aspects of classroom life and became more skilled at seeing students as members of society as well as of their classroom" (p.58). Schwab et al (2004) describe a teacher preparation program with six semesters of progressively challenging field placement experiences. All students are placed in an urban setting, a special education setting and a regular K-12 setting. During the final year, student teachers are placed in one school for 20 hours a week as interns where they are supposed to conduct inquiry into their teaching and share their findings in a yearlong seminar: seminars help students integrate what they are learning in their core classes with their experiences in their clinical setting. This integrated strand provides a structure for professional growth, reflection, inquiry, and leadership throughout the 3 years of the program (Schwab et al 2004).

Student teacher dispositions

Teacher education programs should assess their students' dispositions and ensure that all pre-service teachers obtain dispositions that have a positive impact on children (Flowers, 2006). Gentry (2008) found that pre-service teachers with positive dispositions were more successful in their field placement as shared by a participant who said that her field experiences working with struggling students changed the way she thought about them:

> She developed a desire to help them and saw that they had that spark to learn and complete assignments, and she really enjoyed working with them. This candidate valued classroom-based experience and other opportunities to observe and apply specific practices. (Gentry, 2008, p.13)

Collaboration and feedback from cooperating teachers

Collaborating teachers are the most significant people in the whole process of teacher preparation. Participants in Gentry (2008) study described the act of observing a co-operating teacher as amazing, effective, influential and memorable. Listen to the following:

> Today an amazing thing happened. I saw teaching at its best. She used this demonstration to teach the students how to tell the differences between parallel lines and perpendicular lines. I would recommend participating in educational observations to

143

any students who asked me because the experience gained from such an opportunity is priceless. (Gentry, 2008, p. 17)

My overall experience (at school) was one of the most effective, influential and memorable experiences of my life. Being under the supervision of one of the best teachers I have met thus far, I truly believe that I can become a very effective educator and a productive member of society. (Gentry, 2008, p. 17)

Reflection and problem solving opportunities

Teachers at all levels require effective and sufficient education to be able to adequately carry out their roles and responsibilities. Teachers need the self-confidence to carry out their duties in unique demanding situations and need to implement their expertise in such a way that their customers, stakeholders and colleagues trust them (Isopahkala Brunet, 2004). Working as an expert requires the acquisition of knowledge and practical abilities to work in complex situations with the goal of developing teachers who are reflective, analytic practitioners (Namunga & Otunga, 2012.

Field placement is a significant component of teacher preparation program. The length and quality of placement enables teachers to acquire pedagogical and reflective skills that help them to understand their students. Being provided with opportunities to develop positive dispositions towards the students is significant to the overall student teacher development. Most importantly, having the opportunity to work with the host teachers who have mastered the art of teaching enriches the overall experience of the student teachers. Finally, student teachers need to be provided with opportunities for problem solving. To acquire the analytical skills necessary to solve problems, student teachers need to be exposed to situations where they can practice that art. Even with all this understanding, little is known about the field placement in Kenya and its impact in the overall teacher preparation programs. This study investigated the field experiences of student teachers in a small catholic sponsored college in Uashin Gishu county of Kenya.

Methodology

Setting

During the academic year 2011-2012, I was invited to teach an education foundation course in a small teacher training college in Uasin Gishu district of Kenya. The Catholic sponsored teacher training college (TTC) opened in 2009 with the aim of providing teaching courses to students and at the same time mould them into all-round community leaders. At the time of the study, it had a population of approximately 70 teacher trainees and 10 instructors, most of who were on part time basis. The college offers three kinds of certification as registered by the ministry of education (MOE). There is the primary teachers' education certificate (PTE) which takes two years to complete, the diploma of education which takes three years and the early childhood education certificate which is school-based and only offered during the school holidays. The study focused on the students pursuing the PTE.

According to the MOE guidelines, teacher trainees pursuing the PTE must undertake three teaching practice sessions. One is done when they are in the first year of training and the other two in their second year of training. I was able to be part of the first year training practice session as a supervisor, having taught the class in the first semester of an education foundation course. The training practice was done in a nearby primary school. The teacher trainees were taken to the school by bus every morning where they would take control of the classroom for the morning section and then return to college in the afternoon to prepare for the next day.

Sampling

Twenty two teacher trainees participated in this study. Thirteen were female, eight were male and one was unspecified. The age range of the participants was 20-30 years with a majority below 25 years. This was a convenience sampling having been the instructor of this class for duration of two terms. Except for the questionnaire where students were invited to voluntarily respond, all the other data was collected as part of the required assignments. Nevertheless, the participants were informed that their work may be used towards the study and if they should have any objections, they should contact the instructor before the end of the term. None of the participants objected.

Instruments

A number of instruments were used to collect data for this study as follows: a) observations; b) structured questionnaire; and c) student journals.

Observations: All participants had to be observed at least three times by a college instructor. The instructor was provided with an official form that asked specific questions on the behavior of the teacher trainee. Questions included whether the teacher had good mastery of the content they were teaching, good control of the classroom or use of appropriate methods of teaching. The questions were rated as from 1-10 with 10 being the highest indicator. There was also an open ended question where the instructor could add more comments. Twelve out of the 21 participants were observed using this criterion.

Structured Questionnaires: This instrument was designed to specifically assess the teacher tranee's overall experience after the teaching practice. A number of open ended questions in regard to preparedness in content knowledge, teaching methods and classroom management were asked. In addition, questions regarding support from co-operating teachers and college instructors were included. All the 22 participants voluntarily responded to the questionnaire.

Student Journals: This instrument was part of the required assignment. Teacher trainees were asked to spend at least 10 minutes of their day reflecting on their teaching experience. They had to respond to a prompt of what went well for the day, what went wrong and what they would do differently. The aim of this assignment was to help the students stay connected with the acts and behavior they encountered as classroom teachers. All the 22 participants handed in complete daily reflections for the two weeks they were in the field.

Procedure

I sought and obtained permission from the school principal to collect data for this study during the field placement. Prior to the beginning of the field placement, I supplied each student teacher with a note book and asked them to keep a journal to document their experiences in the field. While they were free to document their experiences for each day in any way they could, I asked them to keep in mind the things that went well for them, things that may not have gone well and what they would do differently. They were expected to have the date for each journal entry and each entry should be at least one page of their note book.

During the time the student teachers were in the field placement, I was able to observe 12 student teachers in two days. Each lesson lasted 35 minutes. I took hand written notes of what was going on throughout the period I was in the classroom but was also required to fill out my assessment of certain teacher behavior as observed. This is the form that was then filed with the college administration as evidence that indeed, the student teachers have fulfilled the mandatory field placement requirement.

146

Immediately after the student teachers completed their field placement, they filled out the structured questionnaire which asked them to document their experiences in the field. They were assured of confidentiality and anonymity of their responses. They all received a cover letter that explained the purpose of the study and its benefits to the future of the program. Participation was voluntary and they could withdraw from the study at any time without penalty.

Results and findings

Physical conditions and infrastructure

The field placement for this TTC took place for two weeks in a government-sponsored school located in a low-income neighbourhood in the outskirts of the major city. To access the school is an all-weather road that makes it extremely difficult for vehicles to get to during the rainy season and even worse during the dry season because of dust. The TP happened in February which is the driest month of the year. The school itself is arranged in a rectangular block with classes next to each other by grade and stream. Somewhere along the block are the administrative office on one side and the staffroom on the adjacent block. The student teachers were given one room for use in preparing their lessons as well as wait for their turn as they were paired up per class. I'm not sure when the school was built but it is obvious that there has never been any renovations since then. The floors that were initially cemented had only remnants of that cement and which have now turned into dusty islands. The windows that may initially have had glass are now shielded from the winds by cardboards made of recycled carton materials. The compound has no tree standing. Needless to say, it is common to have wind and dust cloud the classroom, lifting papers and ripping off the widows. The physical condition of the school was summarized by a student teacher who shared in a journal entry:

> There is this one challenge that is really affecting us though it's natural but it is our prayer that it will stop. It's about the dusty windy. The place is very windy and the wind is accompanied by so much dust. We cannot put our charts on the walls and be sure that they will stay there; they are pulled down by the strong winds. Also we are not able to work well due to the much dust that is revolving around us now and then.

A majority of the student teachers reported that the wind and dust was a distraction to their teaching. Sometimes, the wind would blow through the class bringing in dust and making it impossible

147

to continue with the lesson. Some reported that the wind and dust would affect their health conditions causing allergic reactions to the eyes. This was well summarized by a teacher student who said: "The weather was not good in that it was very dusty and in most cases it was disturbing learners' attention".

Classroom size

The classrooms themselves were overcrowded. It appears each class was built to hold about 40 students. However, each class has now over 70 students. The wooden desks that were meant for maximum four students had to accommodate about six. Desks have also been lined up to the front such that the teacher had only standing space and could hardly move even to check what the students at the back were doing. The difficulties experienced by the student teachers due to overcrowding were well summarized by a student teacher who shared:

> The school is heavily populated in terms of pupils, ranging up to 1300 and in that kind of environment you don't expect to have an easy task because it means having learners up to 70 in a class, and these are all mature minds which need attention, controlling them for anyone even a qualified teacher wouldn't be something to talk gratefully about later.

The teacher students found teaching large classes a real challenge. One student teacher explained that due to the large class, he found it very difficult to control the learners as the only strategy he had was to speak loudly for all of them to hear him. This he found intimidating because he was not used to speaking loudly. Having a large class was made even worse by the fact that the learners had all kinds of abilities. For new teachers to be able to identify and attend to the needs of all the different ability learners was a real challenge. This sentiment was well expressed by a student teacher who said: "Teaching at this school is somehow challenging because it was the first time and there were many learners with different abilities and different background and each learner require different attention". Having to work in an overcrowded classroom brought along other challenges for the student teachers. They were unable to effectively control the classroom. This sentiment was expressed by a participant who said:

> In a class of 67 learners, class control is not a thing to joke about; a ratio of 1:67 needs a lot of effort in maintaining the class control. My biggest challenge here was class control maintenance

which was such a headache. I want to believe that it would/it is a headache to the regular teacher to deal with such numbers.

Instructional resources:

It is obvious looking at the physical conditions of the school that there were inadequate resources in all other areas. But what frustrated the students most was the lack of text books. There is an assumption during the college instruction that the student teachers will find adequate text books that are used regularly in the classroom. To the amazement of the student teachers, some subjects had no text books and even those available had to be shared among students and across classrooms. At the end of one lesson, it was common to see the few textbooks available been collected and shipped to the next classroom. This sentiment was well summarized by a student teacher who shared the following:

> The main issue was mostly on text books whereby learners did not have enough from the library. This made student teacher not to teach well during certain topics that required learners to read a passage on testing reading skills.

The sentiment was further expressed by another student teacher who shared:

> The chalkboard was not in good condition hence I had to give short notes. Some of the learners did not have books or pens hence it made learning difficult. Also in my class there was not enough desks hence the class was very congested. There were not enough books in the school library hence doing more research was difficult and no text books for the learners.

Supervision and feedback

Prior to the beginning of student teaching practice, one day was set aside for observation. During the time of observation, student teachers would meet with their host teacher, get to know the learners as well as the school layout. For the most part, student teachers gained from this experience in terms of general and psychological preparedness. They got to understand the sitting arrangement of the learners, the progress of the work to be covered and the kind of materials they needed to bring to facilitate learning. The host teachers also pointed out for them the effective strategies to use with some of the students with behavioural issues. One participant summarized it well when she said:

I met my regular teacher on the first day of observation, she guided me and had to tell me more about the pupils and how to deal with them, she gave me the guidelines and the professional documents to be used. I took my time to note down the names of the pupils in order to prepare the register and progress records. She also issued out the timetable so I had to compose and make my own copy. The teacher also directed me where to start when I take over in the subjects I was to teach. She gave me textbooks and other teaching material in order to prepare my schemes of work in advance.

Most of the host teachers were quite happy to have the student teachers for those two weeks. A few cooperated with the student teachers and showed them how things are done. A majority of the student teachers reported that their host teachers just disappeared. One student teacher reported that her host teacher gave her a hard time in establishing instruction centres as he had been taught to do at the college. Lack of proper mentoring from host teacher was well summarized by a student teacher who shared: "The only bad experience was that, I didn't get enough support from my regular teacher because she never appeared during my TP."

Other student teachers were also not happy with the host teachers. Some of them disappeared as soon as the student teachers assumed classroom duties. Others were not helpful and student teachers were not mentored as shared by one participant: "I also learned that when you are in that field, you don't even depend on the regular teacher but stand alone as a teacher because the only person you will be seeing is your co-student teachers".

Others were unhappy because the college instructors did not arrive in good time or some did not arrive at all leading to some students not getting assessed at all.

I will only urge the college instructors at least to have time with the student teacher during this session so that consultations are made. Also [it is important that] the documents to be approved in a timely manner. Some tried but others were not available to approve. Whereby some were not approved which can cause confusion.

Professional confidence

Student teachers were proud of what they accomplished during the short time they did the teaching practice. Many of them felt they had gained professional confidence at the end of the T.P. Professional confidence was defined with terms such as gaining courage, establishing rapport with teachers and students, greater ability to communicate with students, improved classroom management among others. Listen to this participant:

On my side I gained courage and changed my attitude towards teaching. Yes, in the beginning I felt that teaching was very difficult and later came to know that it was easy. My learners were able to enjoy my lessons and even after assessing them, they could enjoy my examinations and score well. This encouraged me and I knew that my objectives had been achieved. I had made a good relationship with my learners and even by the time I was completing the teaching practice some were crying [when they heard I was leaving] meaning that I was a good teacher.

Student teachers also found the teaching practice enjoyable for the most part. This was well summarized by a participant who shared thus:

My teaching experience was generally good, and I realised that I can be a good teacher in the future because I just have the courage and the ability to do well and keep on improving. I realized that teaching requires one to have good preparation in mastering the content and preparing the teaching and learning resources for reinforcement of the learners.

And echoed by another who said:
- I liked the whole thing and I really enjoyed interacting with learners.
- I enjoyed the profession of being a teacher and felt proud when learners gave me all the respect.
- As a teacher you are entitled to many challenges so to be called a teacher you need to be fully prepared for anything.

They described themselves as resilient even when the conditions were difficult as share by a participant:

My student teaching practice actually was good despite of the challenges faced. It equipped me with skills, methods and positive attitudes towards learning and courage, mastery of the content as well on how to achieve your set objectives. It also gave me that spirit of being a teacher to help the [education] hungry child to get education in Kenya as well as Africa as a continent.

In summary, student teachers in this study experienced many difficulties some that were weather-related, lack of instructional resources such as textbooks, controlling large classrooms and lack of mentoring from host teachers. These difficulties were summarized well by a student teacher who said:

> There were a lot of difficulties I underwent in this primary school especially the first week. Examples -: most of the regular teachers were not cooperative; weather conditions were tough that is too windy, lack of class textbooks and reference materials and also maintenance of class control.

It made one student teacher describe teaching as indeed a calling because no amount of money would pay for the patience that a teacher had to have.

> I felt that teaching must be a calling and not an interest, since I had to realize that as a teacher you need to have patience and understanding, not anger. In this school I met with more than one thousand students and I had to address [their needs].

Discussion and Conclusion

The purpose of this study was to investigate the effectiveness of a field placement in a primary teacher training college. Field placement and clinical experiences have been said to be the most significant part of teacher preparation programs. It is the period in which student teachers are able to put into practice the theories they have learned in the college classroom. Student teachers in this study found the experience enriching and rewarding. They reported that they had gained professional confidence and had acquired a positive disposition towards the teaching profession. They described themselves as resilient with the abilities to solve problems even in adverse conditions.

However, these findings need to be interpreted with caution. The student teachers in this study were also my students. It is possible they would report what they assumed the instructor would want to hear. The use of triangulation has however minimized this limitation. Even though the sampling was convenience and generalizability cannot be assumed, this study has yielded significant data that deepen our understanding on the importance of field placement in teacher preparation programs.

Student teachers in this study reported enjoyment and professional growth as a result of their student teaching experience. This finding concurs with Flowers (2006) who found that field placements provided student teachers with opportunities for professional growth and positive dispositions. The same sentiments are supported by Gentry

(2008) who also found that field placement enabled student teachers to develop empathy towards their students. It is important to point out that student teachers in this study did find the feedback provided by their college instructors significant. This finding is consistent with Schwab et al (2004) who found that having the field placement linked to a seminar at the college produced better outcomes.

Student teachers in this study experienced many challenges and difficulties within the two weeks placement. The school condition and infrastructure were poor yet the student teachers were able to solve problems and complete their assignments. This level of resilience could be explained by the kind of conditions the students also have to endure in their own homes or even at the college. It could also be explained by the Christian values imparted by the college hidden curriculum. While a few student teachers could be heard grumbling about the condition of the host school and poor infrastructure, a majority persevered and completed their assignments on time.

The field placement for the TTC was only two weeks and one day of prior observation. Yet, the student teachers felt they had acquired a level of professional growth that has had an impact on their general disposition. The student teachers were pretty much on their own once they assumed the role of the classroom teachers. This could be described as a "swim or sink" kind of scenario. Once the host teacher handed out the instructional material, the student teacher had to use their own resources to complete the topics assigned. The host teacher did not have any formal responsibility to assess whether the student teacher had accomplished what they had set out to do. It is therefore difficult to assess accurately whether the student teachers really did accomplish their tasks and if they were successful.

Student teaching does not seem to hold a significant position in the general curriculum of teacher preparation. The college did not feel much obligated to make the student teaching longer because the more important thing is to cover the syllabus where government exams are set. There is little communication between the college administration and the school beside agreement that the school will host student teachers. Certainly, there is no formal responsibility for host teachers to actively mentor and supervise the student teachers.

Field placement is a significant component of teacher preparation programs. The college may want to increase resources in terms of helping the teacher students practice their craft in a place that is environmentally friendly and with some improved infrastructure. While it is obvious the conditions of the school are beyond the control of the college, care must be taken to ensure that student teachers are not assessed based on the conditions of the school which may even turn off even the most positive of the teachers.

Regular teachers should be given a formal role of supervising and mentoring student teachers. While most would take this as an opportunity to take a well-deserved break, leaving the students at the hands of student teachers is a disservice to all involved. The young students take time to acclimate to a new teacher and it would be a great opportunity to help the student teacher transition smoothly in the teaching without worrying too much about the indiscipline and other behavioral issues.

Further research need to be done in the area of teacher reflection and inquiry. While many student teachers identified problems with the physical conditions and inadequate resources, little is known about how they solve pedagogical problems especially as it pertains to teaching students with diverse needs. It would also be interesting to have research conducted on effective strategies for educating students in low economic status neighbourhoods.

Conclusion

There is no doubt that field placement is indeed a significant element of teacher preparation program. Student teachers are provided with an opportunity to grow professionally and acquire positive dispositions towards teaching. They are provided the opportunity to put into practice the theories they have learned in the college classroom. They also get a chance to reflect on their practice and become problem solvers, an important disposition for teachers in the 21st century·

References

Flowers, C. (2006). Confirmatory factor analysis of scores on the clinical experience rubric a measure of dispositions for pre-service teachers. *Educational and Psychological Measurement* Vol. 66:478 DOI: 10.1177/0013164405282458

Floyd, D. & Bodur, Y. (2005). Using case study analysis and case writing to structure clinical experiences in a teacher education program. *The Educational Forum* 70 (49)

Gentry, R. (2008). Teacher preparation beyond the four walls: What clinical experience does to candidates. A Paper Presentation For The Fourth Annual Reaching Out to Mississippi Education in

Action (ROMEA) Conference: Delta State University

Namunga, N. & Otunga, R. (2012). Teacher education as a driver for sustainable development in Kenya. *International Journal of Humanities and Social Science* Vol. 2 No. 5

Schwab, R., Defranco, T. & McGivney-Burelle, J. (2004) Preparing future teacher-leaders: experiences from the University of Connecticut's five-year teacher education program. *Educational Perspectives*, 36, 20-25

Shin, E., Wilkins, E. & Ainsworth, J. (2004). The nature and effectiveness of peer feedback during an early clinical experience in an elementary education program. *Action in Teacher Education* Vol. 28, No. 4

Singh, D. & Stoloff, D. (2006). What do teacher candidates have to say about their clinical experiences? Paper presented at the annual meeting of the Association of Teacher Educators (ATE), Atlanta, GA

Varrati, A. (2008). Making an Impact. *Principal Leadership (Middle Sch Ed)*. Vol. 9 (4)

Wentworth, N., Erickson, L., Lawrence, B., Popham, A & Korth, B. (2009). A paradigm shift toward evidence-based clinical practice: Developing a performance assessment. *Studies in Educational Evaluation*. Vol. 35. 16–20

* 9 7 8 1 9 2 6 9 0 6 3 7 9 *